**this book is from
the kitchen library of**

_____

## ALSO BY ART GINSBURG, MR. FOOD®

The Mr. Food® Cookbook, OOH it's so GOOD!!™ (1990)

Mr. Food® Cooks Like Mama (1992)

Mr. Food® Cooks Chicken (1993)

Mr. Food® Makes Dessert (1993)

Mr. Food® Cooks Real American (1994)

Mr. Food®'s Favorite Cookies (1994)

Mr. Food® Grills It All in a Snap (1995)

Mr. Food®'s Quick and Easy Side Dishes (1995)

Mr. Food®'s Fun Kitchen Tips and Shortcuts (and Recipes, Too!) (1995)

# MR. FOOD®
# cooks
# pasta

## Art Ginsburg
### MR. FOOD®

WILLIAM MORROW AND COMPANY, INC.
new york

Copyright © 1993 by Cogin, Inc.

All rights reserved. No part of this book may be reproduced or utilized in any form or by any means, electronic or mechanical, including photocopying, recording, or by any information storage or retrieval system, without permission in writing from the Publisher. Inquiries should be addressed to Permissions Department, William Morrow and Company, Inc., 1350 Avenue of the Americas, New York, N.Y. 10019.

It is the policy of William Morrow and Company, Inc., and its imprints and affiliates, recognizing the importance of preserving what has been written, to print the books we publish on acid-free paper, and we exert our best efforts to that end.

Library of Congress Cataloging-in-Publication Data

Ginsburg, Art.
Mr. Food® cooks pasta / Art Ginsburg.
p.    cm.
Includes index.
ISBN 0-688-11601-9
1. Cookery (Pasta).    I. Title.
TX809.M17G56 1993
641.8'22—dc20        93-8501
CIP

Printed in the United States of America


18   19   20

BOOK DESIGN BY CHARLOTTE STAUB

*Dedicated to*
*All those in food and on stage*
*Who've worked as hard as I have—*
*And have yet to realize their dreams,*
*as I have*

# acknowledgments

**A**nybody who thinks a cookbook is simply a collection of recipes thrown together should think again!

It's work, by a lot of people. Well, for instance . . .

My wife, Ethel, who not only helps with the recipe testing, but keeps me in line, too.

My son, Steve, who heads up everything for my books and handles everything that I could possibly think of—and everything else, too! He's the real boss.

My daughter-in-law, Carol, and daughter Caryl Gershman, who organize and make sense of the recipes and all of my words. Each time my scattered thoughts come together to become an entertaining, easy-to-follow book . . . it's because of Carol and Caryl.

Linda Rose, Steve Gershman, Alan Roer, Madeline Burgan, and Loriann Bishop, my recipe testers who test and test until we're all certain that the recipes will work every time. Boy, do they have patience!

And Mary Ann Oliver! She types, copies, sorts, and does hundreds of things for us all so that everything comes out right.

Roy Fantel and Tammy Ginsburg, who check up on all of us with their fine-tooth combs.

Chuck Ginsburg, Flo Toppal, Dan Wolk, and Bill Treacy, who make sure that we all have what we need at our fingertips, right when we need it.

I must also thank my agent, Bill Adler, without whose creativity, foresight, and guidance I wouldn't have written my books; and my editor, Maria Guarnaschelli, who, with a smile on her face and in her voice, encourages and supports me as she leads me to book-writing happiness; and Al Marchioni, Phyllis Heller, Skip Dye, and Larry Norton, the gang at William Morrow who push harder for me than I do for myself—they're not only a publishing group, they're dedicated friends.

And there are more! But these people never get their names on the books like I do; they never get the credit they deserve . . . Well, gosh! They just did, and am I glad—'cause to all these guys I owe a really big THANKS!

Thanks, also, to the companies, friends, and viewers who've graciously shared their recipes with me, including:

The National Pasta Association
Sorrento Cheese Co.
Fresh Garlic Association
Thomas J. Lipton Co.
McCormick®/Schilling®
Pace Picante Sauce
The Turkey Store
Borden, Inc.-Gioia
Bertolli USA, Inc.
Sargento Cheese Co., Inc.
Canned Food Information Council
The North Carolina Department of Agriculture
Butterball
*Restaurant Hospitality Magazine*
Linda Gassenheimer, *Dinner in Minutes*
Ethel Ginsburg
Iris Spindel
Barbara McMullen
Michael Cocca
Alan Roer
Joan Talbert
Janet Queeley
Judy Brock
Lana Leone
Tony Colello
The Chinese Chicken Salad recipe was developed by the Hershey Kitchens and provided courtesy of Hershey Foods Corporation.

# contents

# introduction

**W**ho doesn't like pasta? I mean, what kid of any age, from high chair on up, doesn't love "p'sketti"?

Basically, it's flour and water. When you add eggs, it becomes noodles—but I'm grouping it all together here when I say "pasta." And there *is* a lot to say about pasta!

How odd that just a few years ago everybody steered clear of it. It was thought to be fattening and full of starch, not at all solid or nutritious. Well, surprise! Just look at pasta now!

It's the "energy food." It's got those complex carbohydrates that really make it the "good for you" food. Pasta is a lot of other good things, too, besides healthy!

It's QUICK! Whether dried (from a package) or fresh, pasta's ready in no time. And if your sauce, topping, or flavorings are ready, you're eating in minutes. With our busy life-styles today leaving us little time in the kitchen . . . pasta is perfect! It's the best kind of fast food, it's healthy food!

It's a perfect make-ahead item, too, with so many pasta casserole possibilities. There are some new pastas on the market that don't require precooking. I've provided recipes where you don't cook the regular pasta separately (like Tex-Mex Lasagna, page 81). You just put the dish together the night before. Then the liquid ingredients can soak into the pasta and add enough moisture so the pasta cooks through in the oven.

Pasta is VERSATILE! There are pasta soups, side dishes, salads, main dishes, and yes, even desserts. There are pastas with meat, chicken, turkey, seafood, cheese, vegetables, and fruit. It is great for brunch, lunch, dinner, snacks, and if you're like my family . . . even for breakfast! (Well, how many people grab some of their last night's pizza the next morning? There's no difference. We are talking versatility, aren't we?) There are casserole dishes like Four-Cheese Pasta (page 86), Ravioli Lasagna (page 85), and Noodle Pudding (page 132). There are simple pastas and fancy pastas. . . . Now, that's versatile!

Pasta is REASONABLE! In fact, it's probably the best value in town. It's always readily available, and it comes in every shape and size imaginable. From the big lasagna and manicotti shells, down to the tiny shapes, like pastina, it's all always easy-to-find. What makes it an even better value is that our markets always have one or two types of pasta on sale. The pasta manufacturers seem to take turns week by week offering super savings on a few of their shapes. Wouldn't it be nice if we could manage to use that on-sale brand and shape every week? Well, there are enough options in this book to make that possible. Which brand should you go with? You know what you like best. Try them all—from fresh to packaged domestic to imported, all prices and shapes. But if you have a particular preference, go ahead and enjoy it! (Even expensive types are still a great value when you consider our overall food costs today.)

Another part of the super value of pasta is that there's no waste. It can always be reheated. It can be refrigerated in a covered container for up to three days. Then when you want it, just drop it into boiling water again for a minute and drain. Presto! "Fresh" pasta. If it's already mixed with sauce, it's great reheated in a skillet, the oven, or the microwave. Leftover pasta can end up as the noodles in our soup, or maybe as a side dish (with a little more of the original sauce). It can be panfried into a super Spaghetti Pie (page 33). There we go talking versatility again. But that's included in the Reasonable part, too!

Now sure, if you serve your pasta with caviar or tenderloin, it becomes an expensive meal. But that's up to you. You won't find those kinds of recipes in this book, though. There's nothing exotic and expensive here . . . just some creativity with everyday right-from-the-supermarket-shelf items that can look as fancy as you want them to be, without any fancy work. EASY and QUICK, those are the words!

Simply paired with a quick sauce, the recipes here are Fast, Fast! And there are all kinds of sauces in here. From Italy, Spain, China,

Greece, Mexico, the United States, and other places, they're red, orange, green, white, creamy, chunky, fresh, lightly cooked, and long-cooked. (Excuse me, long-cooked-*tasting*.)

Sure, years ago the only sauce was the genuine long-cooked, homemade sauce. Mama's sauce came from the heart . . . can't ever beat that. But now with our better manufacturing—better quality, better packing, better standards—some of today's bottled sauces are *almost* as good as homemade. (See my Note, below, for how to make those even better.)

Yes, pasta means *comfort*. It's the food of home, of family. We're returning to the "back then" foods, like meat loaf, mashed potatoes, Blue Plate Specials, home-tasting breads and muffins . . . and, definitely, pasta. Whatever the reason . . . we want those satisfying, pleasant comforts.

Okay, some of those comforts aren't very weight-conscious. Well, it depends what you want to do with your pasta. These are basic, "as is" recipes. Do whatever you want to make them your own. Where I could, I've made a few suggestions for "lightening up" particular recipes. And if you have a diet restriction, then by all means make your own substitutions, such as less salt, etc. You know what you can and can't have. Check with your doctor, and make these work for you.

With over one hundred delicious, quick and easy recipes, I know for sure that this book won't get a chance to collect dust on your bookshelf. It's gonna be at your elbow, on your counter, ready to add novelty to your meals. Even if you use it just for ideas, that's fine. Any way you do it, you'll still be a kitchen hero! That should make you very happy. And when you're happy, I'm happy, 'cause you know what happy people say . . . Yup,

OOH it's so GOOD!!™

NOTE: With some simple "doctoring," most all bottled sauces can come close to homemade. Here's what to do: Sauté a small chopped onion, ½ a chopped green or red bell pepper, and a crushed garlic clove in 1 tablespoon of olive oil for 3 to 4 minutes. Stir that mixture into your sauce as it's warming. Give it a shot . . . it works!

**introduction**

# charts
## and
# information

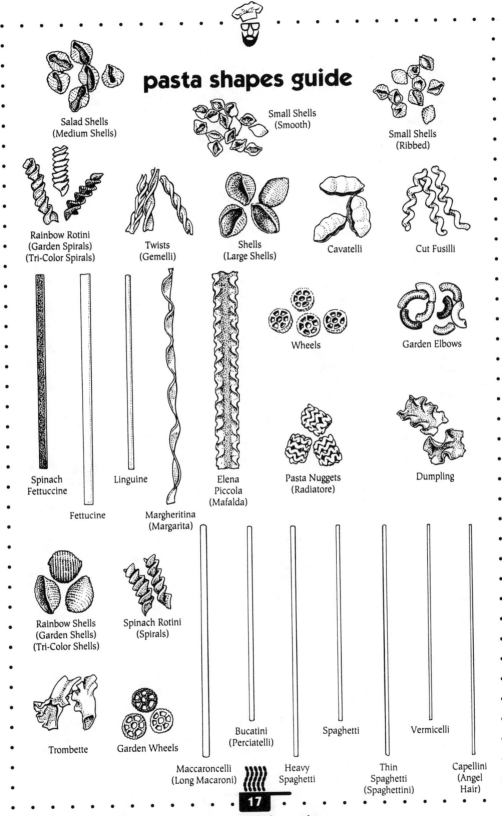

# pasta shapes guide

Salad Shells
(Medium Shells)

Small Shells
(Smooth)

Small Shells
(Ribbed)

Rainbow Rotini
(Garden Spirals)
(Tri-Color Spirals)

Twists
(Gemelli)

Shells
(Large Shells)

Cavatelli

Cut Fusilli

Wheels

Garden Elbows

Spinach
Fettuccine

Fettucine

Linguine

Margheritina
(Margarita)

Elena
Piccola
(Mafalda)

Pasta Nuggets
(Radiatore)

Dumpling

Rainbow Shells
(Garden Shells)
(Tri-Color Shells)

Spinach Rotini
(Spirals)

Trombette

Garden Wheels

Maccaroncelli
(Long Macaroni)

Bucatini
(Perciatelli)

Heavy
Spaghetti

Spaghetti

Thin
Spaghetti
(Spaghettini)

Vermicelli

Capellini
(Angel
Hair)

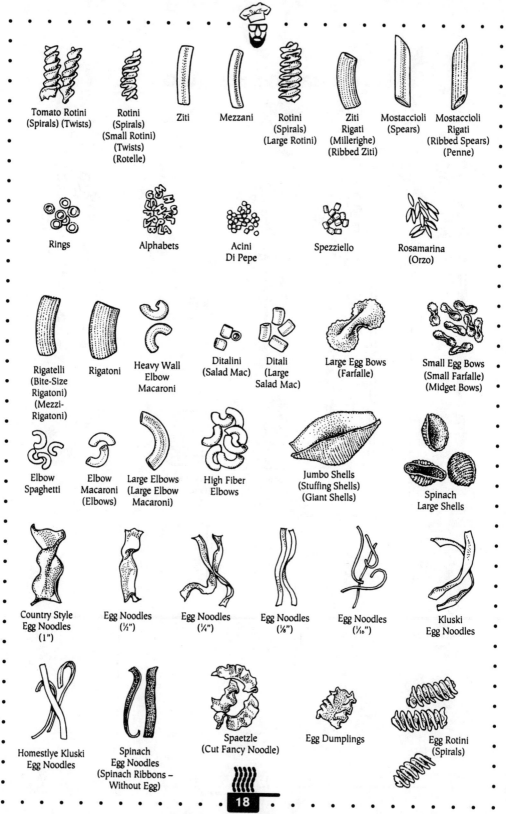

Tomato Rotini
(Spirals) (Twists)

Rotini
(Spirals)
(Small Rotini)
(Twists)
(Rotelle)

Ziti

Mezzani

Rotini
(Spirals)
(Large Rotini)

Ziti
Rigati
(Millerighe)
(Ribbed Ziti)

Mostaccioli
(Spears)

Mostaccioli
Rigati
(Ribbed Spears)
(Penne)

Rings

Alphabets

Acini
Di Pepe

Spezziello

Rosamarina
(Orzo)

Rigatelli
(Bite-Size
Rigatoni)
(Mezzi-
Rigatoni)

Rigatoni

Heavy Wall
Elbow
Macaroni

Ditalini
(Salad Mac)

Ditali
(Large
Salad Mac)

Large Egg Bows
(Farfalle)

Small Egg Bows
(Small Farfalle)
(Midget Bows)

Elbow
Spaghetti

Elbow
Macaroni
(Elbows)

Large Elbows
(Large Elbow
Macaroni)

High Fiber
Elbows

Jumbo Shells
(Stuffing Shells)
(Giant Shells)

Spinach
Large Shells

Country Style
Egg Noodles
(1")

Egg Noodles
(½")

Egg Noodles
(¼")

Egg Noodles
(⅛")

Egg Noodles
(¹⁄₁₆")

Kluski
Egg Noodles

Homestlye Kluski
Egg Noodles

Spinach
Egg Noodles
(Spinach Ribbons –
Without Egg)

Spaetzle
(Cut Fancy Noodle)

Egg Dumplings

Egg Rotini
(Spirals)

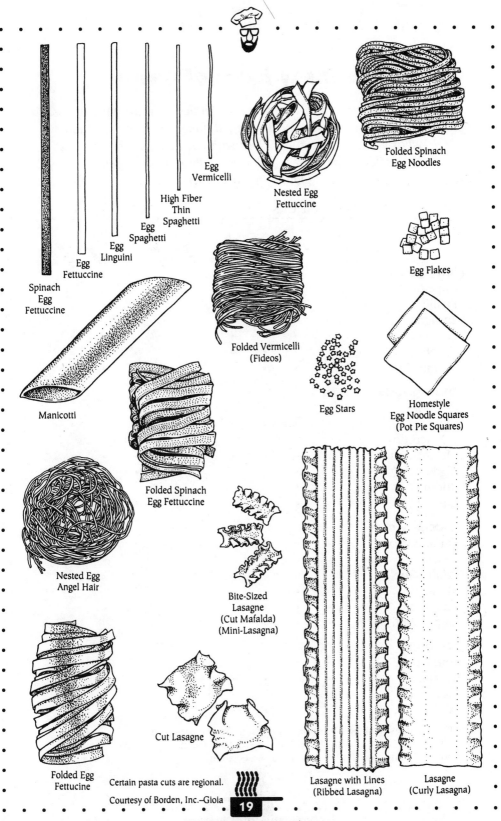

Spinach Egg Fettuccine

Egg Fettuccine

Egg Linguini

Egg Spaghetti

High Fiber Thin Spaghetti

Egg Vermicelli

Nested Egg Fettuccine

Folded Spinach Egg Noodles

Egg Flakes

Folded Vermicelli (Fideos)

Egg Stars

Homestyle Egg Noodle Squares (Pot Pie Squares)

Manicotti

Folded Spinach Egg Fettuccine

Nested Egg Angel Hair

Bite-Sized Lasagne (Cut Mafalda) (Mini-Lasagna)

Folded Egg Fettucine

Certain pasta cuts are regional.

Courtesy of Borden, Inc.–Gioia

Cut Lasagne

Lasagne with Lines (Ribbed Lasagna)

Lasagne (Curly Lasagna)

**charts and information**

# the many faces of pasta

*This easy-to-use chart provides a few guidelines on what types of pasta are best for soups, salads, stir-fries, stuffings, or casseroles, and what kinds of sauces work best with each shape. The chart includes the most popular pasta shapes which can be easily found in most supermarkets.*

| | SAUCES | | | | USES | | | | | |
| --- | --- | --- | --- | --- | --- | --- | --- | --- | --- | --- |
| | Cream or Cheese | Meat | Tomato | Oil or Butter | Soup | Salad | Stuffing | Casseroles | Stir-fry | Top with sauce |
| **long goods** | | | | | | | | | | |
| Capellini* | | | • | • | • | • | | | • | • |
| Fusilli | • | • | • | • | | | | | • | • |
| Lasagna | • | • | • | | | | | • | | |
| Linguine* | • | • | • | • | • | | | | • | • |
| Spaghetti* | • | • | • | • | • | | | • | | • |
| Vermicelli* | • | • | | | • | | | | • | • |
| **short goods** | | | | | | | | | | |
| Ditalini | • | • | • | | • | • | | • | | |
| Elbow Macaroni | • | • | • | | • | • | | • | | • |
| Mostaccioli | • | • | • | • | | • | | • | • | • |
| Rigatoni | | • | • | • | | | | • | • | • |
| Rotini | • | • | • | • | | • | | • | • | • |
| Ziti | • | • | • | • | • | | | • | | • |
| **specialty cuts** | | | | | | | | | | |
| Farfalle (Bow ties) | • | • | • | • | • | • | | | | |
| Jumbo Shells | • | • | • | | | | • | • | | |
| Manicotti | • | • | • | | | | • | • | | |
| Radiatore | • | • | • | • | | • | | • | • | • |
| Small Shells | • | • | • | • | • | • | | • | | • |
| **noodles** | | | | | | | | | | |
| Fettuccine | • | • | • | • | | • | | | | • |
| Medium Noodles | • | • | • | | | | | • | | • |
| Wide Noodles | • | • | • | • | | | | • | | |

*These shapes work best in soups if broken in half before cooking.

NOTE: Rigati is not a pasta shape, but rather a term meaning "grooved."

SOURCE: Courtesy of the National Pasta Association.

# pasta "particulars"

**D**id you know that *pasta* is the Italian word for "paste"? It's called that because it's made from a mixture of wheat flour and water, and sometimes eggs, too.

There are many myths and mysteries surrounding the beginnings of pasta, but the Italians, Egyptians, Greeks, and Chinese each claim it as their own.

No matter where it originated, the National Pasta Association says that "pasta possibilities are endless"! They offer these interesting ideas for "expanding your food repertoire with pasta":

Buy a new pasta shape each time you shop. If you always buy pasta shells, try long strands, tubes, different colors, even a bag of mixed shapes and colors.

If you're cautious about cholesterol, use vegetable toppings and sauces that contain no dietary cholesterol. Add fresh chopped tomatoes, or liven up canned tomatoes with sliced mushrooms and a splash of wine—maybe even add some chopped chives.

Improve the nutrient value of your basic pasta sauces: Add red or green bell peppers, or broccoli, all high in vitamins A and C, to tomato or marinara sauces. Use parsley, also high in vitamins A and C, as a major ingredient, not just as a garnish. Add some garbanzo beans, red kidney beans, lima beans, or black beans to a tomato sauce to increase fiber and protein.

## cooking pasta

Generally, cook pasta in a large pot of boiling salted water, allowing about 1 quart of water for every ¼ pound of pasta. Slip pasta into the

boiling water, a little at a time, so that the water keeps boiling. Stir immediately so pasta doesn't stick together!

Fresh pasta cooks quickly, usually in just 2 to 3 minutes; dried pasta takes between 7 and 12 minutes. Always check the specific package directions.

Stir pasta occasionally, checking for doneness. Cook it to desired doneness (see my note on Pasta Doneness), and drain.

Time your sauce so that it is ready as the pasta finishes cooking to avoid having the pasta become soft and gluey while waiting. If using it in salad, rinse it in cold water after draining.

## pasta doneness

Though pasta can be cooked to whatever point you want, most every pasta aficionado claims that pasta should be cooked "al dente," which literally means "to the tooth."

When you cook pasta too long, it absorbs the maximum amount of cooking liquid. As a result, when sauce is added, the dish can become weepy or watery. Pasta that is still a little firm is more likely to absorb some of the liquid from the sauce, thus preventing a soggy finished dish. And if you're planning to further cook the pasta, such as in a dish of baked Lasagna, make sure the pasta is even a little firmer.

To determine if pasta is done: Test it by cutting a piece with a fork, or taking a bite. When the pasta has only a slight bit of uncooked core, it is al dente.

When pasta is al dente, it gives you something to chew. I like it that way, but many people like their pasta soft. That's fine, too. Whatever makes us happy!

## lasagna tips

Since it's so popular, there are lots of lasagna recipes here. There's no right way to make it, and any way you make it, it's still a time saver. Try my secrets:

Assemble the lasagna ahead of time. Cover and chill it. Then add 5 to 10 minutes to the baking time. Or take off the chill by microwaving it for a few minutes while preheating your oven.

Freeze unbaked lasagna by double-wrapping it and placing it into a freezer bag. It's the perfect emergency meal for company. Cover it with foil and allow it to bake slowly if putting it into the oven still frozen.

Baked or unbaked, slice individual portions before freezing. This makes it easy for your family to reheat single portions in the oven or microwave for quick dinners.

After removing lasagna from the oven, let it sit for about 10 minutes before cutting.

# quick pasta recipe chart: meals in minutes

*Since pasta is so versatile, you should always have some on hand. And chances are, you're going to have at least a few of the items listed below. If you're willing to experiment, you can have a meal in minutes . . . and a different one every time!*

**B**oil and drain 8 ounces (½ pound) of your favorite pasta. Mix it with one ingredient from each column in the chart below to make about 3 to 4 servings.

| MEAT/FISH | VEGETABLES | SAUCE | SPICE |
|---|---|---|---|
| *Use any one meat/fish in the quantity listed* | *Use any one or any combination of vegetables totaling 2 cups* | *Use any one sauce in the quantity listed* | *Use ½ to 1 teaspoon or to taste (or as indicated)* |
| 1 lb. ground beef, cooked & drained | red bell pepper, chopped or strips | 2 cups bottled spaghetti sauce* | basil leaves |
| 1 lb. ground lamb, cooked & drained | green bell pepper, chopped or strips | ¾ cup Italian dressing | curry powder |
| 1 lb. ground veal, cooked & drained | yellow bell pepper, chopped or strips | ½ cup Italian dressing + ⅓ cup sour cream or yogurt† | dill weed |
| 1 lb. bulk sausage, cooked & drained | broccoli florets | ½ cup olive oil* | Italian seasoning |
| 1 lb. ground pork, cooked & drained | cabbage, chopped or sliced | ½ cup mayonnaise + ⅓ cup sour cream or yogurt† | marjoram leaves |
| 8 to 10 slices bacon, cooked & drained | carrot, sliced, shredded, diced, or julienne | ½ cup olive oil + ¼ cup red wine vinegar | oregano leaves |
| 2 cups cubed fully cooked ham | cauliflorets | 1 15-ounce can flavored or plain tomato sauce* | herbed salt substitutes |
| 2 cups cubed cooked chicken | celery, chopped or sliced | 1 (10¾-ounce) can of any flavor cream soup + ½ cup milk* | seasoned salt |
| 2 cups cubed cooked turkey | cucumber, chopped or sliced† | 1 (11-ounce) can Cheddar cheese soup* | summer savory leaves |
| 2 cups julienne or sliced cooked bratwurst | green onion, sliced | | tarragon leaves |
| | lettuce, torn† | | thyme leaves |
| | olives, sliced | | 1 to 2 cloves garlic, minced |
| | onion, chopped or sliced | | ⅛ to ¼ tsp. garlic powder |
| | | | ¼ to ½ tsp. onion powder |
| | | | ¼ tsp. pepper |

| MEAT/FISH | VEGETABLES | SAUCE | SPICE |
|---|---|---|---|
| *Use any one meat/fish in the quantity listed* | *Use any one or any combination of vegetables totaling 2 cups* | *Use any one sauce in the quantity listed* | *Use ½ to 1 teaspoon or to taste (or as indicated)* |
| 2 cups julienne, cubed, or sliced smoked sausage | tomato, seeded, chopped | 1 (10¾-ounce) can tomato soup* | "Extras" (as desired): bay leaf‡, parsley, Parmesan cheese, raisins, shredded cheese, nuts |
| 1½ cups cubed, sliced, or chopped pepperoni | yellow summer squash, sliced or strips | 2 cups tomato juice* | |
| 1½ cups cubed, sliced, or chopped salami | zucchini, sliced or strips | 2 cups vegetable juice cocktail* | |
| 1 or 2 (6½-ounce) cans tuna, drained | fresh or canned (drained) sliced mushrooms | | |
| 1 or 2 (6½-ounce) cans boneless salmon, drained | canned garbanzo beans, drained | | |
| 1 or 2 (6¾-ounce) cans boneless chicken, drained | canned kidney beans, drained | | |
| 1 or 2 (6½-ounce) cans clams, drained | canned or thawed frozen vegetable combination, drained | | |
| 1½ cups canned or thawed frozen cooked shrimp | canned or thawed frozen corn, drained | | |
| 1 or 2 (6½-ounce) cans crab, drained | canned or thawed frozen peas, drained | | |
| 1 lb. scallops, cooked & drained | canned or thawed frozen green beans, drained | | |
| | thawed frozen chopped broccoli* | | |
| | thawed frozen chopped spinach* | | |

*For hot recipes only.
†For cold recipes only.
‡Always remove bay leaf before serving; therefore, do not use in casseroles or other such dishes.
SOURCE: Courtesy of Borden Pasta Group, Gioia/Creamette.

**charts and information**

# quick measures

|  | EQUALS |
|---|---|
| Dash | less than ⅛ teaspoon |
| 3 teaspoons | 1 tablespoon |
| 4 tablespoons | ¼ cup |
| 5 tablespoons plus 1 teaspoon | ⅓ cup |
| 8 tablespoons | ½ cup |
| 10 tablespoons plus 2 teaspoons | ⅔ cup |
| 12 tablespoons | ¾ cup |
| 16 tablespoons | 1 cup |
| 2 tablespoons | 1 fluid ounce |
| 1 cup | ½ pint or 8 fluid ounces |
| 2 cups | 1 pint or 16 fluid ounces |
| 4 cups | 2 pints or 1 quart or 32 fluid ounces |
| 4 quarts | 1 gallon or 128 fluid ounces |
| Juice of 1 lemon | about 3 tablespoons |
| Grated peel of 1 lemon | about 1½ teaspoons |

# substitutions

| | EQUALS |
|---|---|
| 1 tablespoon dehydrated minced onion | ¼ cup finely minced fresh onion |
| 1 teaspoon onion powder | ⅓ of an onion |
| ⅛ teaspoon garlic powder | 1 garlic clove |
| 1 tablespoon dehydrated parsley flakes | 2 tablespoons fresh minced parsley |

# packaged foods note

**A**s with many processed foods, package sizes may vary by brand. Generally, the sizes indicated in these recipes are average sizes. If you can't find the exact indicated package size, whatever package is closest in size will usually do the trick. Remember that a 12-ounce box of uncooked pasta equals approximately 5 cups cooked.

# pasta appetizers and side dishes

# easy pasta meatballs

### 24 meatballs

*Not your usual meatballs, but I'll bet they get just as*
*many raves. Try them—they're a nice change.*
*Great attention-getters, too.*

| | |
|---|---|
| ½ teaspoon minced garlic | ¼ teaspoon curry powder |
| ¼ cup grated Parmesan cheese | ¼ teaspoon ground ginger |
| 1 cup tiny pasta shape, like pastina or acine di pepe | 1 medium-sized onion, finely chopped |
| 1 pound ground turkey or veal | 1 jar (28 to 29 ounces) spaghetti sauce |
| 1 teaspoon salt | |
| ¼ teaspoon pepper | ½ cup water |

**P**reheat the oven to 325°F. In a large bowl, combine all the
ingredients except the spaghetti sauce and water. Mix together,
then form into 24 golf ball–sized meatballs and place on a foil-
lined cookie sheet that has been coated with nonstick vegetable
spray. Bake the meatballs for 8 to 10 minutes, or until brown, then
immediately spoon them into a 2-quart casserole. In another large
bowl, combine the spaghetti sauce and water; pour over the meatballs. Cover the casserole and bake for 30 to 40 minutes, turning
the meatballs occasionally.

NOTE: Serve as an hors d'oeuvre, or over pasta as a main dish.

**pasta appetizers and side dishes**

# tomato pastina pie

6 to 8 servings

*I say this serves 6 to 8, but, honestly, I could eat the
whole thing myself. It's so good, I can't believe
I got it from an in-law!*

2 teaspoons Dijon-style
mustard

1 frozen 9-inch pie shell,
thawed according to package
directions

2 cups (8 ounces) shredded
mozzarella cheese, divided

¼ cup tiny pasta shape, like
pastina or acine di pepe

1 can (28 ounces) whole
tomatoes, broken up,
undrained

½ teaspoon Italian seasoning

⅛ teaspoon pepper

¼ teaspoon garlic powder

**P**reheat the oven to 350°F. Spread the mustard on the bottom
of the thawed pie shell. Distribute 1 cup of the mozzarella cheese
over the mustard, then the pasta, tomatoes, and seasonings. Top
with the remaining 1 cup mozzarella cheese. Bake for about 40
minutes or until golden. Allow to stand for 10 minutes before
serving.

NOTE: You can prepare this a few hours before mealtime, cover
and refrigerate it, then bake it just before serving.

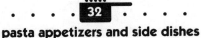

**pasta appetizers and side dishes**

# spaghetti pie

6 servings

*There's something irresistible about this dish that keeps me
coming back for more . . . maybe it's the crunchy outside
and the smooth inside. It reminds me of how Mama
used to turn leftover spaghetti into a reward.*

½ pound cooked spaghetti

2 tablespoons olive oil or
melted butter

2 large eggs, well beaten

½ cup plus 2 tablespoons
grated Parmesan cheese,
divided

1 cup ricotta cheese

1 cup spaghetti sauce

½ cup (2 ounces) shredded
mozzarella cheese

**P**reheat the oven to 350°F. In a large bowl, toss the hot spaghetti with the olive oil. In a small bowl, combine the eggs and the
½ cup of Parmesan cheese. Stir into the spaghetti. Pour the spaghetti mixture into a lightly greased 10-inch pie plate and form into
a "crust." Spread the ricotta evenly over the crust, but not quite to
the edge, and top with the spaghetti sauce. Bake, uncovered, for
25 minutes. Top with the shredded mozzarella. Bake for 5 minutes
more, or until the cheese melts. Remove from the oven and sprinkle
with the remaining 2 tablespoons of Parmesan. Cool for 10 minutes
before cutting into wedges.

**pasta appetizers and side dishes**

# golden ravioli
20 pieces

*Here's a different way to enjoy everybody's favorite. Serving
these as an appetizer or hors d'oeuvre, you can't go wrong,
'cause somebody else did the work of making the ravioli.
You simply finish them off and take the credit.*

1 package (about 20 ounces)
  frozen ravioli
¾ cup flavored bread crumbs
¾ teaspoon garlic powder
¾ teaspoon salt
¼ teaspoon dried basil

¼ teaspoon dried oregano
¼ cup milk
1 egg, beaten
½ cup vegetable oil for frying
2 tablespoons grated
  Parmesan cheese
Spaghetti sauce, for dipping

In a large pot of boiling salted water, cook the ravioli to desired
doneness; drain, pat dry, and cool slightly. Meanwhile, in a medium-sized bowl, combine the bread crumbs, garlic powder, salt,
basil, and oregano; set aside. In another bowl, mix together the
milk and egg. Dip the ravioli, a few at a time, into the milk-egg
mixture to coat, then into the bread crumb mixture to coat. In a
large skillet, heat the oil. Fry the ravioli, a few at a time, until
golden; drain on paper towels. Cover; chill. When ready to serve,
preheat the oven to 350°F. Arrange the ravioli on a baking sheet
in a single layer; sprinkle the Parmesan cheese on top. Bake for
15 minutes, or until heated through. Serve hot with spaghetti sauce
for dipping.

# "hot or not" ziti with sun-dried tomatoes

about 6 servings

*This will be the hit of your party—and the great thing is that
if you're not sure just when your guests will arrive, or if
you're taking it along on a picnic, you won't have to worry!
It can be served warm or at room temperature
(that's actually how I prefer it).
Either way, it's as rich as can be.*

| | | | |
|---|---|---|---|
| 1 | pound ziti | 2 | cups chicken broth |
| ½ | cup olive oil | ½ | cup ricotta cheese |
| 2 | garlic cloves, crushed | ½ | cup grated Parmesan cheese |
| 1 | package (3 ounces) sun-dried tomatoes, blanched and slivered | ½ | teaspoon salt |
| | | 2 | teaspoons pepper |
| | | ½ | cup chopped fresh parsley |

In a large pot of boiling salted water, cook the ziti to desired doneness; drain and place in a large bowl. Meanwhile, in a large skillet, heat the olive oil over medium heat; add the garlic and sauté for about 1 minute. Add the slivered sun-dried tomatoes and sauté for about 1 to 2 minutes more. Stir in the chicken broth and cook just to heat the mixture. Remove the tomato-broth mixture from the heat and pour over the ziti. Add the remaining ingredients, toss until well blended, and serve.

# orzo primavera

about 8 servings

*Here's a light and tasty way to enjoy vegetables and pasta—
all in one easy side dish. The rice-shaped orzo makes it so
"upscale" that you can serve it with anything from meat
to fish to poultry and become a real hero!*

| | |
|---|---|
| 7 cups water | 1 package (10 ounces) frozen peas and carrots combination, thawed |
| 3½ cups chicken broth, divided | |
| 1 pound orzo, acini di pepe, or other small pasta shape | ¼ teaspoon salt |
| | ⅛ teaspoon pepper |
| ¼ cup chopped parsley | ½ teaspoon onion powder |
| | ½ teaspoon minced garlic |

In a large pot, combine the water and 3 cups of the chicken broth and bring to a boil. Add the pasta and cook just until tender; drain. In a medium-sized bowl, combine the pasta with the parsley, peas and carrots, and the remaining ½ cup of chicken broth; toss gently. Add the salt, pepper, onion powder, and garlic; mix to blend thoroughly. Serve warm.

# sunday night noodles

6 servings

*Of course, you can enjoy this dish any time, but I call it
"Sunday Night" because it's light and easy and uses
lots of extras that I usually have on hand
at the end of the weekend.*

| | |
|---|---|
| 1 pound medium egg noodles | 1½ teaspoons salt |
| 1 package (10 ounces) frozen chopped spinach, thawed and drained | ½ teaspoon pepper |
| | 1 teaspoon Italian seasoning |
| 2 cups (1 pound) cottage cheese | 1 tablespoon butter or margarine, melted |
| ½ cup grated Parmesan cheese | ¼ cup dry bread crumbs |
| 1 cup (½ pint) sour cream | |

**P**reheat the oven to 350°F. In a large pot of boiling salted water, cook the noodles to desired doneness; drain. In a large bowl, mix the thawed spinach, cottage cheese, Parmesan cheese, sour cream, salt, pepper, and Italian seasoning. Stir in the noodles. Spoon the mixture into a 9" × 13" baking pan that has been coated with nonstick vegetable spray. In a small bowl, combine the melted butter and bread crumbs. Sprinkle over the noodle mixture. Bake, covered, for 45 minutes.

NOTE: For variety, you can add chopped parsley, scallions, dill, or caraway seed. Do your own thing!

**pasta appetizers and side dishes**

# baked macaroni and eggplant neapolitan

6 to 8 servings

*This is like having a sumptuous side dish of eggplant
parmigiana—without all the work!*

Olive oil for frying

1 medium-sized eggplant,
peeled and thinly sliced

1 jar (26 to 28 ounces)
spaghetti sauce, divided

½ pound rotini or ziti, cooked
and drained

2 cups (8 ounces) shredded
mozzarella cheese, divided

⅓ cup grated Parmesan
cheese, divided

**P**reheat the oven to 425°F. In a large skillet, heat enough oil
to cook the eggplant, a few slices at a time, until well browned;
add oil as needed. Drain the eggplant on paper towels; keep warm.
Reserve 1 cup of the spaghetti sauce; combine the remaining sauce
with the cooked pasta. In a 2-quart baking dish that has been
coated with nonstick vegetable spray, layer half the pasta mixture, ¾ cup mozzarella cheese, half the eggplant, and 2 tablespoons Parmesan cheese; repeat. Top with the reserved spaghetti
sauce and remaining cheeses. Bake, uncovered, for 15 minutes,
or until hot.

# pasta "pizza"

### 6 to 8 servings

*The only strange thing about this one is the name—*
*it's colorful, tasty, and so easy,*
*'cause everything gets layered just like*
*regular pizza, but over a pasta "crust"*
*instead of pizza dough.*

1   pound elbow macaroni or other medium pasta shape

1   tablespoon Italian seasoning

2   garlic cloves, minced

½   teaspoon crushed red pepper

1   can (8 ounces) tomato sauce

¼   cup grated Parmesan cheese

1   can (15 ounces) crushed tomatoes or 2 cups chopped fresh tomatoes

2   cups any combination of chopped fresh vegetables, like celery, onions, red and green bell peppers, zucchini, carrots, spinach, or parsley

½   cup canned chick peas, rinsed and drained

6   pitted ripe olives, sliced (optional)

1   cup (4 ounces) shredded mozzarella cheese

**P**reheat the oven to 400°F. In a large pot of boiling salted water, cook the pasta until just underdone; drain. Place the pasta in a 9" × 13" baking pan that has been coated with nonstick vegetable spray; toss with the Italian seasoning, garlic, crushed red pepper, tomato sauce, and Parmesan cheese. Pour the crushed tomatoes over the top, then layer the remaining ingredients, ending with the mozzarella cheese. Bake for 25 to 30 minutes and serve.

**pasta appetizers and side dishes**

# pasta stuffing

about 8 servings

*Pasta in stuffing? Sure, why not? And once you taste it,
it's likely to become a family favorite. Especially
with the raves you'll get . . .*

8   ounces any small pasta
    shape, like acine di pepe
¼   cup (½ stick) butter or
    margarine
½   cup finely chopped onion

½   cup finely chopped celery
1½  cups hot chicken broth or
    hot water
1   package (7 ounces) herb-
    seasoned stuffing mix or
    cornbread stuffing mix (4
    cups)

**P**reheat the oven to 400°F. In a large pot of boiling salted water, cook the pasta until just underdone; drain and place into a large bowl. Meanwhile, in a large skillet, heat the butter over medium heat; sauté the onion and celery until translucent and mix with the pasta. Add the remaining ingredients and mix together until well blended. Place in a greased 9" × 13" baking pan and bake for 15 to 20 minutes, or until light golden.

NOTE: To make Italian pasta stuffing, prepare the Pasta Stuffing, then add to it ½ pound sautéed hot Italian sausage that has been broken into small pieces and cooked through, 1 minced garlic clove, 1 jar or can (about 4 ounces) sliced mushrooms, drained, and ¼ cup chopped parsley.

**pasta appetizers and side dishes**

# garlic pasta
about 3 servings

*This will fill your house with great aroma, your tummy with fulfillment, and your ears with ooh's and aah's.*

½ pound (about 3 cups) uncooked spiral or twist pasta

¼ cup olive oil

3 garlic cloves, minced

¼ cup finely chopped fresh parsley

Pinch of crushed red pepper

Salt to taste

Black pepper to taste

⅓ cup grated Parmesan cheese

In a large pot of boiling salted water, cook the pasta to desired doneness; drain and place in a large bowl. Meanwhile, in a large skillet, heat the oil over a medium-high heat; add the garlic and sauté until golden brown. Remove from the stove top and mix in the parsley, red pepper, salt, and black pepper. Add the mixture to the pasta, tossing until well coated. Add the Parmesan cheese and toss again. Serve hot.

# pasta soups and stews

# pasta e fagioli
## (pasta and beans)

about 4 servings

*I got this terrific pasta and bean soup from an Italian friend of
mine. It's the real thing, and is it ever good and hearty!
Sure, there are lots of other family favorite ways
to make it . . . but this is one easy version
we love to "throw" together.*

| | | | |
|---|---|---|---|
| ¼ | cup olive or vegetable oil | 1 | teaspoon salt |
| 4 | garlic cloves, coarsely chopped | 1 | teaspoon garlic powder |
| 1 | can (14½ ounces) whole tomatoes, broken up | 2 | cans (15 ounces each) cannellini beans |
| 1 | tablespoon dried oregano | ½ | cup chopped fresh parsley |
| 1½ | to 2 teaspoons pepper | ½ | pound ditalini pasta |
| | | ¼ | cup grated Parmesan cheese |

In a large saucepan, heat the oil over medium-high heat; add
the garlic and sauté until golden. Allow to cool slightly to prevent
splattering, then add the tomatoes, oregano, pepper, salt, and garlic
powder. Reduce the heat to medium and cook for 10 minutes, stirring frequently. Add the cannellini and parsley and continue cooking for 10 minutes more, stirring frequently. Meanwhile, in a
medium-sized pot of boiling salted water, cook the ditalini until
just barely tender; drain and add to the cannellini mixture. Add
the Parmesan cheese, mix thoroughly, and serve.

# minestrone

12 servings
(about 15 cups)

*There are a million different versions of this famous
Italian soup—all good.
Here's a classic, easy recipe that'll give you
a potful of "delicious" and "warm."*

3 quarts (12 cups) beef stock

1 pound cooked beef, cubed

1 cup small pasta shells

1 onion, peeled and chopped

1 potato, peeled and chopped

3 carrots, peeled and chopped

1 package (9 ounces) frozen green beans, thawed

1 package (10 ounces) frozen broccoli spears, thawed and cut into chunks

1 can (15 ounces) kidney beans, undrained

Chopped parsley

Salt to taste

Pepper to taste

Grated Parmesan cheese, for topping (optional)

In a soup pot, combine the beef stock, beef, pasta, onion, potatoes, and carrots. Bring to a boil, then lower the heat and simmer for 45 minutes. Add the green beans, broccoli, and kidney beans and simmer for 15 minutes more. Season with parsley, salt, and pepper. Serve topped with Parmesan cheese, if desired.

# chicorina soup

8 to 10 servings

*If you didn't grow up on this soup, you'll want to start making up for lost time! It's a little different because of the last-minute addition of the egg and cheese mixture.*

MEATBALLS

1 pound ground beef

¼ cup coarsely chopped fresh parsley

2 eggs

1 teaspoon salt

1 to 1½ teaspoons pepper

¾ cup dry bread crumbs

1½ teaspoons garlic powder

½ cup grated Parmesan cheese

SOUP

3 quarts chicken stock

1 garlic clove, chopped

½ cup chopped onion

2 fresh tomatoes, chopped

1½ cups coarsely chopped carrots

1½ cups coarsely chopped celery, with the leaves

¼ teaspoon pepper

¼ cup coarsely chopped fresh parsley

1 box (10 ounces) frozen spinach

1 cup rosamarina pasta

2 eggs, beaten

¼ cup grated Parmesan cheese

In a large bowl, combine all the meatball ingredients. Form the mixture into about 30 small meatballs; set aside. In a large pot, bring the chicken stock to a boil. Add the garlic, onion, tomatoes, carrots, celery, pepper, and parsley; reduce the heat and simmer until the vegetables are tender, about 10 minutes. Add the spinach, meatballs, and rosamarina pasta and continue to simmer until the meatballs are cooked through, 15 to 20 minutes. Meanwhile, in a small bowl, mix together the eggs and Parmesan cheese. Return the soup to a boil, add the egg-cheese mixture, and let boil for 1 minute, stirring gently.

NOTE: This soup is a good one to make in advance. If it's too thick after storing, just add additional chicken stock.

# egg noodle vegetable chowder

4 to 6 servings

*When they ask for seconds (and maybe even thirds)*
*of this pasta soup,*
*you'll be glad to give it to them, 'cause you'll know*
*it's loaded with lots of good things.*

½  pound egg noodles

1  cup diagonally sliced celery

1  small yellow squash, thinly sliced

1  cup fresh broccoli florets

½  cup thinly sliced red onion

2½ cups milk

2  cans (10½ ounces each) condensed chicken broth

1  cup (4 ounces) grated Cheddar cheese

¼  teaspoon salt

¼  teaspoon freshly ground black pepper

In a large pot of boiling salted water, cook the noodles to desired doneness; drain and set aside. Meanwhile, in a large saucepan, combine the vegetables, milk, and chicken broth. Cover and bring to just under a boil. Reduce the heat and simmer for 15 minutes. Stir in the Cheddar cheese, salt, and pepper. Add the noodles to the vegetable mixture. Simmer for about 5 minutes or until thoroughly heated.

# chick pea and pasta soup

6 to 8 servings

*I feel warm all over just thinking about this. Try it . . . and
you and your gang will see
that it'll easily do the same for you.*

1 tablespoon vegetable oil

1 garlic clove, minced

2 onions, chopped

1 can (15 ounces) chick peas

5 cups chicken broth

1 cup ditalini or any medium
   pasta shape

½ teaspoon salt

½ teaspoon pepper

1¾ cups chopped cooked
   chicken meat (about 2
   boned and skinned
   chicken breasts)

In a large saucepan, heat the oil over medium heat; sauté the garlic and onions for about 5 minutes (do not brown). Add the chick peas, chicken broth, pasta, salt, pepper, and chicken. Cook for 10 to 15 minutes, or until the pasta is tender; serve.

NOTE: You can use dark chicken meat, if you prefer.

# easy italian chicken noodle soup

4 to 6 servings

*Who doesn't enjoy a bowl of fresh homemade soup? Here's a tomato-y chicken soup that's a meal in itself.*

- 2 tablespoons vegetable oil
- 2 celery stalks, thinly sliced
- 1 medium-sized onion, thinly sliced
- 2 carrots, thinly sliced in rounds
- 2 cans (10½ ounces each) condensed chicken broth
- 2 soup cans cold water
- 1 can (14½ ounces) whole tomatoes, coarsely chopped, undrained
- 8 ounces egg noodles or other small pasta shape
- 2 cups cooked chicken or turkey, chopped
- 2 tablespoons finely chopped fresh parsley
- ¼ teaspoon dried thyme leaves
- ¼ teaspoon salt
- ¼ teaspoon pepper

**H**eat the oil in a large saucepan; add the celery, onion, and carrots and sauté over medium heat, stirring occasionally until the vegetables are tender-crisp. Add the chicken broth, water, and tomatoes and simmer for 15 to 20 minutes, or until the carrots are tender. Increase the heat slightly and stir in the pasta. Cook for about 6 minutes, until the pasta is tender, stirring occasionally. Add the chicken, heat through, and season with the parsley, thyme, salt, and pepper. Serve.

# easy vegetable chicken noodle soup

8 to 10 servings

*Nothing is more welcome than a nice, big bowl of soup.*
*Here's a really rich whole-meal feast your family's gonna*
*thank you for!*

2 tablespoons vegetable oil

2 garlic cloves, minced

1 medium-sized onion, chopped

4 medium-sized carrots, sliced

2 cups fresh broccoli florets

2 cups sliced fresh mushrooms

1 cup sliced celery

4 cups water

4 cans (10½ ounces each) condensed chicken broth

1 teaspoon dried dillweed

Salt to taste

Pepper to taste

2 cups chopped cooked chicken (about 2 boned and skinned chicken breasts)

8 ounces egg noodles or other medium pasta shape

In a large pot or Dutch oven, heat the oil over medium-high heat; add the garlic and onion and sauté until the onion is tender. Add the remaining ingredients, except the pasta, and bring to a boil. Reduce the heat and simmer for 20 minutes. Meanwhile, in a large pot of boiling salted water, cook pasta to desired doneness; drain and stir into the soup. Heat through and serve.

# quick spaghetti beef soup

8 to 10 servings

*If you want leftovers for tomorrow (or the freezer),*
*you'd better make extra,*
*'cause you're gonna keep hearing,*
*"One more bowl, please!"*

1 pound ground beef

1 package (16 ounces) frozen mixed soup vegetables or mixed vegetables

4 cups vegetable juice cocktail or tomato juice

4 cups water

2 tablespoons instant beef bouillon

1 teaspoon dried basil leaves

1 teaspoon dried thyme leaves

1 teaspoon salt

½ teaspoon onion salt

½ teaspoon pepper

¼ teaspoon garlic powder

2 tablespoons Worcestershire sauce

½ pound spaghetti, broken into thirds

Grated Parmesan cheese (optional)

In a soup pot or Dutch oven, brown the ground beef over medium-high heat; drain off the fat. Stir in the mixed vegetables, vegetable juice cocktail, water, beef bouillon, basil, thyme, salt, onion salt, pepper, garlic powder, and Worcestershire sauce; bring to a boil. Reduce the heat and simmer for 30 minutes. Meanwhile, in a large pot of boiling salted water, cook the spaghetti to desired doneness; drain. Add the spaghetti to the soup mixture; heat through. Serve with Parmesan cheese.

# meatball and shells stew

3 to 4 servings

*Remember when Italian tomato sauce used to slow-cook
on Mom's stove for hours and hours?
Well, here's a way to get that same satisfying,
good taste—but in a jiffy!*

MEATBALLS

½ pound ground beef

¼ cup uncooked long
grain rice

1 egg, beaten

⅛ teaspoon pepper

2½ cups water

1 envelope onion soup mix
(from a 2-ounce box)

¼ teaspoon dried thyme
leaves

1 can (14½ ounces) whole
tomatoes, broken up

¼ teaspoon garlic powder

½ teaspoon Italian seasoning

½ cup small shell pasta

In a medium-sized bowl, combine the meatball ingredients. Shape the mixture into 1-inch meatballs and place on a cookie sheet or a piece of waxed paper; set aside. In a medium-sized saucepan, combine the water, onion soup mix, thyme, tomatoes, garlic powder, and Italian seasoning; bring the mixture to a boil. Carefully drop the meatballs and shells into the boiling mixture; reduce heat and simmer, covered, for 25 minutes.

NOTE: I sometimes like to use ground turkey or chicken for a lighter change. You can even add cut-up fresh or frozen veggies.

# pasta salads

# gazpacho pasta salad

about 6 servings

*This is great as is, or you could really get adventurous
and add more hot pepper sauce for some extra zip!*

½ pound elbow macaroni or
any medium pasta shape

4 medium-sized ripe tomatoes,
seeded and chopped

½ cup sliced scallion

½ cup cucumber, peeled,
seeded, and chopped

¼ cup grated Parmesan cheese

Dash of hot pepper sauce

1 garlic clove, minced

2 tablespoons chopped
parsley

½ cup vegetable oil

1 tablespoon wine vinegar

1 teaspoon salt

½ teaspoon black pepper

Cayenne pepper to taste

1 can (6 ounces) spicy
vegetable juice

In a large pot of boiling salted water, cook the pasta to desired doneness; drain and place in a large bowl. Add the remaining ingredients and combine until thoroughly mixed. Cover and chill for at least 1 hour, then mix again before serving.

# summer pasta salad

about 10 servings

*This is one of those salads that's just right for
so many things—a patio party,
family picnic, lunch—you get the picture.
The only reason I call it "summer" is 'cause it makes me
feel as good as summer does.*

2 cups ditalini or other small pasta shape

1 package (16 ounces) frozen mixed vegetables, thawed and drained

¼ cup finely chopped onion

⅔ cup mayonnaise

2 tablespoons lemon juice

2 teaspoons sugar

1 teaspoon dried dillweed

1 teaspoon salt

¼ teaspoon pepper

In a medium-sized pot of boiling salted water, cook the pasta to desired doneness; drain well and cool. (Rinse with cold water to cool quickly; drain well.) In a large bowl, combine the cooled pasta, mixed vegetables, and onion; mix well. In a small bowl, combine the mayonnaise, lemon juice, sugar, dillweed, salt, and pepper; blend well. Pour the mayonnaise mixture over the pasta-vegetable mixture; toss lightly. Chill before serving.

NOTE: Garnish with paprika and serve over lettuce, if desired. If you're not serving the salad immediately, add an additional ¼ cup mayonnaise to moisten just before serving. If you'd like to make this a hearty main course, add a cup of cooked chicken or beef or some diced cheese.

# greek pasta salad

about 10 servings

*For a minute, I thought I was getting a whiff of Mediterranean Sea air. Well, this salad does just that.*

1   box (14 to 16 ounces) radiatore or pasta ruffles

1   bag (10 ounces) fresh spinach, rinsed and coarsely chopped

½   pound (8 ounces) feta cheese, crumbled

½   cup Italian dressing

½   cup vegetable oil

1   tablespoon chopped fresh basil or 1½ teaspoons dried basil

1   tablespoon grated Parmesan cheese

1   tablespoon wine vinegar

¼   teaspoon salt

¼   teaspoon pepper

In a large pot of boiling salted water, cook the pasta to desired doneness; drain and cool immediately by rinsing in cold water, then drain again. Meanwhile, in a large bowl, mix together all the remaining ingredients thoroughly but gently; add the pasta and toss. Serve or refrigerate until ready to serve (best when served at room temperature).

# pasta primo

8 to 12 servings

*I love pasta, so I'm always happy to find new ways to enjoy it. Here's an easy pasta salad that's a meal in itself. (And you know how popular pasta salad is!)*

1 package (12 ounces) twist rainbow pasta

1 package (16 ounces) frozen broccoli, cauliflower, and carrot combination, thawed

½ cup Italian dressing

1 teaspoon dried oregano

1 teaspoon dried basil

¼ teaspoon garlic powder

½ cup (2 to 3 ounces) chopped pepperoni

½ cup mayonnaise

In a large pot of boiling salted water, cook the pasta to desired doneness; drain and cool. Meanwhile, in a large bowl, mix together the remaining ingredients until well blended. Toss the pasta with the vegetable mixture; serve chilled.

NOTE: This is great made in advance, but you may need to add a little extra Italian dressing to moisten it just before serving.

# peppy pasta salad

9 to 12 servings

*Last-minute company? Last-minute picnic?*
*Last-minute anything?*
*Then you'll be glad you can whip up this pasta salad in a*
*hurry ('cause they'll think it took you a long time to make it!).*
*It's got a nice touch of Southwest flavor, too.*

1 box (12 ounces) tricolor twist pasta

1 bag (16 ounces) frozen carrot, cauliflower, and broccoli combination, thawed and drained

1 bottle (8 ounces) picante sauce

3 tablespoons mayonnaise

1 tablespoon finely chopped onion

¼ teaspoon garlic powder

¼ teaspoon salt

¼ teaspoon pepper

In a large pot of boiling water, cook the pasta to desired doneness; drain and allow to cool. In a large bowl, mix together the remaining ingredients until thoroughly combined; toss in the pasta. Serve immediately or refrigerate until ready to serve.

NOTE: Even if you're *planning* on making this, go ahead and make it in advance—but if you do, you may want to moisten it with a little extra mayonnaise just before serving. You can add your favorite seasonings, too. And if you like your veggies more tender, go ahead and blanch them first.

# athenian pasta salad

8 to 10 servings

*Have you noticed how the tastes of Greece
are getting so popular?
Now you know what one of my all-time favorite
summer lunches is.
(In fact, I like it in the spring, fall, and winter, too!)*

| | | | |
|---|---|---|---|
| 1 | pound twist or any medium pasta shape | 2 | small tomatoes, chopped |
| ½ | cup finely chopped red onion | ¾ | cup vegetable oil |
| | | 6 | tablespoons red wine vinegar |
| 1 | cup ripe olives, chopped | 1½ | teaspoons salt |
| 8 | ounces (about 2 cups) crumbled feta cheese | ½ | teaspoon black pepper |
| | | 1 | teaspoon sugar |
| ¼ | cup finely chopped green bell pepper | 2 | teaspoons Dijon-style mustard |

**I**n a large pot of boiling salted water, cook the pasta to desired doneness; drain, cool, and place in a large bowl. Add the onion, olives, feta cheese, green pepper, and tomatoes. In a small bowl, whisk together the remaining ingredients; pour over the pasta and toss gently. Refrigerate until ready to serve.

# fresh fruit shell salad

10 servings

*What a nice fresh taste this has! It's great for lots of things,
from lunch, to a snack, to dessert . . .
mostly dessert. It's especially nice
to have this ready in the fridge for the kids to
"grab and snack"—and they do. (Of course, don't
tell them it's good for them.)*

½ pound shells or other
medium pasta shape

1 container (8 ounces) plain
low-fat or nonfat yogurt

¼ cup frozen concentrate
orange juice, thawed

1 can (20 ounces) pineapple
chunks in juice, drained

1 large orange, peeled,
sectioned, and seeded

1 cup seedless red grapes, cut
into halves

1 cup seedless green grapes,
cut into halves

1 apple, cored and chopped

1 banana, sliced

In a large pot of boiling salted water, cook the pasta to desired
doneness; drain and set aside. In a small bowl, mix the yogurt and
orange juice concentrate. In a large bowl, combine the fruit. Add
the yogurt mixture and pasta; toss to coat. Cover; chill thoroughly.
Toss gently before serving. Refrigerate leftovers.

# twist turkey salad

4 to 6 servings

*Here's another way to combine some favorites
(healthy ones, too!).
And you talk about easy!!*

| | |
|---|---|
| ½ pound twist pasta or any medium pasta shape | ⅓ cup vegetable oil |
| | 2 tablespoons cider vinegar |
| 1½ cups chunked cooked turkey or chicken (about 2 boned and skinned chicken breasts) | ½ teaspoon dried thyme leaves |
| | ½ teaspoon dried dillweed |
| | ½ teaspoon garlic powder |
| ¼ medium-sized onion, finely chopped | 1 teaspoon salt |
| | ¼ teaspoon pepper |
| 1 package (10 ounces) frozen peas and carrots combination, thawed | 1 teaspoon sugar |

**I**n a large pot of boiling salted water, cook the pasta to desired doneness; drain. Meanwhile, in a large bowl, combine the turkey and vegetables. Add the pasta. In a small bowl or jar, combine the remaining ingredients; mix or shake until well blended, then pour over the pasta mixture and mix well. Cover and chill until ready to serve, mixing occasionally.

# chicken and vegetable pasta salad

8 to 12 servings

*So colorful and wonderfully fresh-tasting—it'll have everyone coming back for seconds.*

| | |
|---|---|
| 12 ounces tricolor spiral pasta | 2 cooked chicken breasts, skinned, boned, and cut into bite-sized chunks |
| 1½ cups mayonnaise | |
| 1 cup grated Parmesan cheese | 1 cup chopped tomato |
| ½ cup milk | 1 cup chopped green bell pepper |
| 1 teaspoon salt | ¼ cup coarsely chopped onion |

In a large pot of boiling salted water, cook the pasta to desired doneness; drain, let cool, and set aside. Meanwhile, in a large bowl, combine the mayonnaise, Parmesan cheese, milk, and salt. Add the pasta and toss to blend. Mix in the remaining ingredients. Chill for several hours before serving.

NOTE: You may need to moisten the salad with additional mayonnaise just before serving.

# chicken and tortellini pesto

6 to 8 servings

*This is no ordinary pasta salad. Simply serve it over salad greens for a taste and a look that can't be beat.*

1 pound cheese tortellini

1 pound cooked boneless chicken breast, cubed

⅓ cup vegetable oil

½ cup Italian dressing

¼ cup chopped parsley

¼ cup chopped fresh basil

¼ cup grated Parmesan cheese

About ½ cup Pesto Sauce

In a large pot of boiling salted water, cook the tortellini to desired doneness; drain and cool immediately by rinsing in cold water, then drain again. In a large bowl, mix together all the ingredients thoroughly but gently.

NOTE: Any store-bought pesto will work fine, or you can make your own (page 152).

# chicken macaroni salad

about 12 servings

*Here's a bit of a twist on an old favorite—and
the chicken makes it
substantial enough to be a complete meal. In fact, it is!*

| | |
|---|---|
| 1 pound elbow macaroni | 4 cups chunked cooked chicken |
| 6 large eggs, hard-boiled and chopped | 1 teaspoon salt |
| 1 cup chopped celery | 1 teaspoon pepper |
| 2 cups mayonnaise | |

In a large pot of boiling salted water, cook the macaroni to desired doneness; drain and cool. In a large bowl, mix together all the ingredients and serve or chill until ready to serve.

NOTE: You may want to moisten this with additional mayonnaise before serving, if you've chilled it first. For a different taste, try adding 1 teaspoon dried dillweed or dried basil, or ½ teaspoon celery seed.

# picnic pasta

12 to 15 servings

*This does make a great picnic lunch, but I confess that I don't always wait 'til I go on a picnic to enjoy it!*

| | |
|---|---|
| 1 | pound small pasta shape, like small shells or elbows |
| 3 | cups cooked chicken, diced (about 3 boned and skinned chicken breasts) |
| 2 | cups frozen peas, thawed |
| 2 | bunches scallions, chopped |
| ½ | head iceberg lettuce, cut into 1-inch chunks |

CREAMY CHILI DRESSING

| | |
|---|---|
| 1½ | cups mayonnaise |
| 1 | cup chili sauce |
| ¼ | cup lemon juice |
| 1 | tablespoon chopped fresh parsley |
| 1 | teaspoon pepper |
| 2 | large tomatoes, cut into wedges, for garnish |

In a large pot of boiling salted water, cook the pasta to desired doneness; drain. In a medium-sized bowl, toss together the pasta, chicken, peas, scallions, and lettuce. In a food processor or blender, mix together the dressing ingredients until smooth. Gently blend the dressing into the pasta salad. Place the pasta salad in a serving bowl or on a platter and garnish with tomato wedges.

NOTE: You'll have about 2½ cups dressing. If you make this in advance, mix the dressing with the pasta mixture just before serving.

# st. louis horseradish salad

10 to 12 servings

*I don't know why it's called St. Louis, but I do know that it has zip! What a nice touch of novelty!*

1 pound rigatoni or other medium pasta shape

1 pound skinless cooked chicken, shredded

1 teaspoon salt

½ teaspoon pepper

1 tablespoon sugar

2 teaspoons dried dillweed

3 celery stalks, chopped

1 cup sliced mushrooms

2 scallions, chopped

3 tablespoons Dijon-style mustard

2 tablespoons prepared horseradish

5 tablespoons vegetable oil

4 tablespoons white vinegar

In a large pot of boiling salted water, cook the pasta to desired doneness; drain and place in a large bowl. Add the chicken to the pasta, season with salt, pepper, sugar, and dillweed, then combine with the celery, mushrooms, and scallions. In a small bowl, combine the mustard, horseradish, vegetable oil, and vinegar. Add to the pasta and toss gently. Serve immediately or refrigerate and serve chilled.

# chinese chicken salad

4 to 6 servings

*Have some leftover chicken, but not enough for another meal? Here's a great way to s-t-r-e-t-c-h it! And today, everybody's really enjoying Asian flavorings.*

- ⅓ cup soy sauce
- 1 tablespoon prepared mustard
- 1½ tablespoons vegetable or sesame oil
- 2 cups (about 2 boned and skinned chicken breasts) cooked chicken, cut into thin strips
- 1 cup elbow macaroni
- 1 package (6 to 8 ounces) frozen snow peas, thawed and drained
- ½ cup sliced scallion
- ½ cup (about ½ an 8-ounce can) water chestnuts, drained, or chopped celery
- Chow mein noodles, for garnish

In a medium-sized bowl, blend the soy sauce, mustard, and oil; add the chicken and toss lightly until well coated. Chill for about ½ hour, to blend flavors. Meanwhile, in a large pot of boiling salted water, cook the macaroni to desired doneness; drain well. Let cool (or rinse with cold water to cool quickly, then drain well). Drain the chicken, place in a large bowl, then combine gently with the cooled macaroni, snow peas, scallion, and water chestnuts until blended. Serve immediately or chill. Garnish with chow mein noodles.

NOTE: This is good served on a bed of lettuce.

# tuna twist

8 to 10 servings

*There are so many new ways to prepare pasta salad, but this
old-fashioned tried-and-true way of mine is still
one of my all-time favorites.*

½ pound elbow macaroni

2  cups mayonnaise

¼ cup cider vinegar

Dash of pepper

1  can (6½ ounces) tuna,
   drained and flaked

2  cups frozen peas, thawed

2  cups sliced celery

1  cup chopped red onion

½ cup snipped fresh dill or 3
   to 4 tablespoons dried
   dillweed

In a medium-sized pot of boiling salted water, cook the macaroni to desired doneness; drain and place in a large bowl. In a
small bowl, mix together the mayonnaise and cider vinegar until
smooth; add to the macaroni and gently stir together until well
blended. Add the remaining ingredients and toss to coat well.
Cover and chill.

# veal and pesto pasta salad

3 to 4 servings (about 4 cups)

*Three special ingredients add up to one great taste—and some simple touches can make it a special summer delight. (I made this when I was catering. Everybody loved it!)*

1 pound veal stew meat, cut into small cubes

½ pound uncooked small macaroni shells

½ cup Pesto Sauce

In a pot of boiling salted water, cook the veal for about 10 to 15 minutes, or until done. Meanwhile, in another pot of boiling salted water, cook the macaroni to desired doneness; drain and cool well. Place the macaroni in a large bowl and add the veal cubes; add the pesto sauce and toss to thoroughly coat the veal and macaroni. Serve at room temperature but if making in advance, keep refrigerated and toss with a bit more pesto sauce just before serving.

NOTE: This is nice served over shredded romaine or other salad greens, with tomato slices. Sprinkle lightly with Parmesan cheese, if desired. Any store-bought pesto will work fine, or you can make your own (see recipe on page 152).

# taco pasta salad

6 to 8 servings

*Two favorite flavors come together to make one great dish!*
*It's got the "today populars" . . . in a snap!*

½ pound elbow macaroni or any medium pasta shape

1 pound ground beef

1 package (1¼ ounces) taco seasoning mix

¾ cup water

1 tomato, chopped

½ medium-sized onion, finely chopped

1 cup (4 ounces) shredded Cheddar cheese

½ cup pitted black olives, chopped

¾ cup taco sauce or salsa

1 medium-sized head iceberg lettuce, shredded

1 avocado, peeled and cubed, for topping

Crushed corn chips, for topping

In a large pot of boiling salted water, cook the pasta to desired doneness; drain, cool, and place in a large bowl. In a large skillet, over medium-high heat, brown the beef, stirring to break it up, until no pink remains; drain off the fat, then add the taco seasoning mix and ¾ cup water. Stir; bring to a boil, then reduce the heat and simmer, uncovered, for about 10 minutes. Add the beef mixture, tomato, onion, Cheddar cheese, and olives to the pasta; toss gently. Add the taco sauce and mix gently. Serve on a bed of shredded lettuce, topped with avocado and crushed corn chips. Serve cold or warm.

# beefed-up mostaccioli salad

about 6 servings

*This is my idea of great picnic basket food. In fact, anytime*
*you want that open, airy, "alfresco" feeling . . . this'll do it.*

DRESSING

½ cup vegetable oil

¼ cup red wine vinegar

2 tablespoons grated Parmesan cheese

2 garlic cloves, minced

1 teaspoon Dijon-style mustard

1½ teaspoons salt

1 teaspoon dried oregano

½ teaspoon pepper

3 cups mostaccioli or other similar pasta shape, like penne

1 pound cooked roast beef, cut into julienne strips

1 package (9 ounces) frozen green beans, thawed

2 small tomatoes, chopped

¼ cup chopped scallion

In a small bowl, combine the dressing ingredients; mix well. In a large pot of boiling salted water, cook the mostaccioli to desired doneness; drain. In a large bowl, combine the mostaccioli, roast beef, green beans, tomatoes, and scallion. Pour the dressing over the pasta mixture; toss to coat. Chill until ready to serve.

# shells with broccoli

4 to 6 servings

*Close your eyes and you're in the south of Italy! Well, not quite, but this is a popular way to enjoy pasta the way Southern Italians do.*

| | | | |
|---|---|---|---|
| 5 | tablespoons olive oil | 1 | pound shell pasta shape |
| 2 | garlic cloves, minced | 1 | head broccoli, cut into florets with 1-inch stems |
| ½ | teaspoon dried basil | | |
| ½ | teaspoon dried oregano | ¼ | pound pepperoni, diced |
| 1½ | teaspoons salt | 2 | tablespoons grated Parmesan or Romano cheese |

Pinch of crushed red pepper (optional)

In a small skillet, heat the olive oil over low heat until warm; stir in the garlic, basil, oregano, salt, and red pepper; cook, stirring, until the garlic is soft, about 5 minutes (do not let the garlic brown). Meanwhile, in a large pot of boiling salted water, cook the pasta and broccoli, stirring, for 10 to 13 minutes, or until the pasta and broccoli are tender. Drain the pasta and broccoli, reserving ½ cup of the cooking water. Place the pasta in a large bowl. Toss with the garlic mixture, the reserved cooking water, and pepperoni. Sprinkle with grated cheese and serve.

# pasta main courses

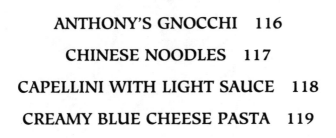

# tex-mex lasagna

about 6 servings

*This has become a family favorite because of the popularity of Tex-Mex. It has that little different touch that raises eyebrows. (And we don't have to cook the noodles first . . . yup, that's right. They go in uncooked—you'll see.)*

SAUCE

1 pound ground beef

½ cup chopped onion

1 cup tomato paste (1 6-ounce can contains about ⅔ cup)

1 cup picante sauce (medium or mild)

¾ cup water

1 teaspoon dried oregano

1 teaspoon dried basil

1 cup ricotta or cottage cheese

2¼ cups shredded mozzarella cheese, divided (2 cups equals 8 ounces)

½ pound (½ of a 16-ounce box) uncooked lasagna noodles

In a large skillet, make the sauce by browning the beef with the onion; drain the liquid. Add the tomato paste, picante sauce, water, oregano, and basil; mix well and set aside. In a large bowl, combine the ricotta cheese and ¾ cup of the mozzarella cheese; set aside. Coat a 7" × 11" baking pan with nonstick vegetable spray. Layer the ingredients in the pan as follows: ⅓ cup of the sauce, half of the uncooked lasagna noodles, and half of the ricotta cheese mixture; repeat the same layers and top with the remaining sauce, then the remaining 1½ cups mozzarella cheese. Cover and refrigerate overnight. The next day, uncover and bake in a preheated 350°F. oven for 1 hour, or until light golden. Remove from the oven and let stand for 20 minutes for easier serving.

# turkey lasagna

6 to 8 servings

*Here's a different way to enjoy our old favorite—'cause it's much lighter, yet just as tasty and "happy making"!*

10 strips lasagna noodles (a 16-ounce box of lasagna contains about 20 strips)

1 cup (4 ounces) shredded mozzarella cheese

1 cup ricotta cheese

¼ cup grated Parmesan cheese

2 tablespoons vegetable oil

1 pound ground turkey

1 garlic clove, crushed

1 can (4 ounces) mushroom pieces and stems, undrained

1⅔ cups spaghetti sauce (a 28-ounce jar contains 3 cups)

4 to 5 slices mozzarella cheese, for topping

**P**reheat the oven to 350°F. In a large pot of boiling salted water, cook the lasagna noodles to desired doneness; drain, rinse, and pat dry. Meanwhile, in a small bowl, combine the mozzarella cheese, ricotta cheese, and Parmesan cheese; set aside. In a large skillet, heat the oil; add the ground turkey and brown. Add the garlic, mushrooms, and spaghetti sauce; bring to a boil, reduce the heat, and simmer for 5 to 10 minutes. Pour about a third of the meat mixture into a greased 9" × 13" baking pan. Add a layer of lasagna strips, then pour another third of the meat mixture over it. Carefully spread half the cheese mixture on top. Add another layer of lasagna strips, the remaining meat mixture, and the remaining cheese mixture. Top with mozzarella slices. Bake for 25 to 30 minutes, or until golden brown. Let set for 15 minutes before cutting into serving-sized pieces.

# spinach mushroom lasagna

6 to 8 servings

*Spinach and mushrooms combine to make this a
great-tasting meatless lasagna.*

1 container (15 ounces) ricotta
cheese

1 egg

1 package (8 ounces) shredded
mozzarella cheese, divided

1 jar (28 ounces) spaghetti
sauce

½ pound (½ of a 16-ounce
box) uncooked lasagna
noodles

1 box (10 ounces) frozen
chopped spinach, thawed
and drained

2 cups sliced fresh
mushrooms

1 cup water, divided

**P**reheat the oven to 350°F. In a medium-sized bowl, combine
the ricotta cheese, egg, and 1 cup of the shredded mozzarella
cheese; set aside. Pour half of the spaghetti sauce on the bottom
of a 9" × 13" baking dish that has been coated with nonstick vegetable spray. Cover the sauce with half of the uncooked noodles;
spread the cheese mixture over the noodles, then layer over that
the spinach, mushrooms, the remaining cup of shredded mozzarella cheese, remaining noodles, and remaining sauce. Pour ¼ cup
of water into each corner of the pan. Cover tightly with aluminum
foil and bake for 1¼ hours. Do not unseal the top until cooking
time is complete. Remove from the oven, uncover, and let stand
for 10 to 15 minutes before serving.

# broccoli lasagna

about 8 servings

*Now you can "lighten up" your lasagna and use it as a side
dish, for lunch, brunch, or that Sunday night "perfect."
This meatless one is sure to be a big hit!
(Especially with you, 'cause you
don't have to boil the lasagna noodles!)*

1   container (15 ounces)
    ricotta cheese

1½  cups (6 ounces) shredded
    mozzarella cheese, divided

1   large egg

1   package (10 ounces) frozen
    chopped broccoli, thawed
    and drained

1   teaspoon salt

¼   teaspoon pepper

¾   teaspoon dried oregano

1   teaspoon chopped garlic

¾   teaspoon dried basil

1   jar (28 ounces) spaghetti
    sauce

½   pound (½ of a 16-ounce
    box) uncooked lasagna
    noodles

1   cup water

**P**reheat the oven to 350°F. In a large bowl, mix together the
ricotta cheese, 1 cup of the mozzarella cheese, egg, broccoli, salt,
pepper, oregano, garlic, and basil. In a greased 9" × 13" baking
pan, layer ½ cup of the spaghetti sauce, a third of the noodles,
and half of the cheese mixture. Repeat the layers and top with the
remaining noodles, then the remaining sauce. Sprinkle with the remaining ½ cup of mozzarella cheese. Pour water around the edges,
cover tightly with aluminum foil, and bake for 1¼ hours, or until
bubbly. Let stand for 15 minutes before serving.

# ravioli lasagna

about 8 servings

*Wondering why you never thought of this? It sure is
an easy shortcut to an all-time favorite.
(Using the ravioli sure cuts down
on the shopping.)*

| | |
|---|---|
| 2 bags (about 20 ounces each) square ravioli | 3 tablespoons grated Parmesan cheese |
| 4¾ cups spaghetti sauce, divided (1 28-ounce jar contains about 3 cups) | 3 cups (12 ounces) shredded mozzarella cheese |

**P**reheat the oven to 350°F. In a large pot of boiling salted water, cook ravioli to desired doneness; drain. Pour 1 cup of the spaghetti sauce on the bottom of a 9" × 13" baking dish, layer a third of the ravioli on top of the sauce, sprinkle with 1 tablespoon Parmesan cheese, pour 1¼ cups of sauce over it, then cover with 1 cup of the mozzarella cheese. Repeat the layers two more times. Bake for 35 to 40 minutes, or until golden. Cool for 15 minutes before serving.

# four-cheese pasta

6 to 8 servings

*Gooey, rich, and bubbly—if you're a cheese lover, you'll love this. Plenty of full, cheesy flavor here!*

½ pound ziti or bow ties

2 tablespoons vegetable oil

¼ cup finely chopped onion

3 cups chopped canned tomatoes, drained (1 28-ounce can contains about 2 cups)

1 teaspoon dried basil

¼ teaspoon salt

½ teaspoon pepper

1 cup ricotta cheese

4 slices mozzarella cheese

4 slices Swiss cheese

6 slices provolone cheese

**P**reheat the oven to 350°F. In a large pot of boiling salted water, cook the pasta to desired doneness; drain. In a large saucepan, heat the oil over medium-high heat. Add the onion, reduce the heat to low, and cook, stirring occasionally, until just soft (do not brown). Stir in the tomatoes, basil, salt, and pepper. Cook, uncovered, for 5 to 10 minutes. Remove from the heat and set aside to cool slightly. Spoon a thin layer of the tomato mixture into a 9" × 13" baking pan that has been coated with nonstick vegetable spray. Layer with a third of the pasta, all the ricotta cheese, all the mozzarella cheese, another third of the pasta, all the Swiss cheese, the remaining pasta, and the sauce. Top with the provolone cheese. Cover and bake for 30 minutes, or until mixture is hot and bubbly. Let set for 10 minutes before serving.

# baked manicotti

6 to 8 servings

*If it's old-time raves you want, this is your guarantee.*

14 manicotti (8-ounce package) or 35 to 40 large pasta shells (12-ounce package) for stuffing

1 large container (32 ounces) ricotta cheese

3 cups (12 ounces) shredded mozzarella cheese, divided

½ cup plus 2 tablespoons grated Parmesan or Romano cheese, divided

2 eggs, beaten

1 tablespoon chopped fresh parsley

1 teaspoon crushed garlic

1 teaspoon salt

½ teaspoon pepper

3 cups spaghetti sauce

**P**reheat the oven to 350°F. In a large pot of boiling salted water, cook the pasta until just barely tender, about 5 to 6 minutes. Drain, cover with cold water, then drain again. In a large bowl, mix together the ricotta cheese, 2 cups of the mozzarella cheese, the ½ cup of Parmesan cheese, eggs, parsley, garlic, salt, and pepper. Pour ½ cup of the spaghetti sauce onto the bottom of each of 2 lightly greased 8-inch square glass baking dishes. Fill each manicotti or shell generously with the cheese mixture. Place the filled pasta in the prepared baking dishes. Pour 1 cup of the spaghetti sauce over each baking dish, then top each baking dish with ½ cup of the shredded mozzarella and 1 tablespoon Parmesan. Bake for 40 to 45 minutes, or until light golden. Let set for 10 minutes before serving.

NOTE: An easy, efficient way to fill the pasta is to carefully place the cheese mixture in a large resealable plastic storage bag with a corner snipped off; then squeeze the filling into the pasta, using the storage bag like a pastry bag.

**pasta main courses**

# my own italian meatballs

12 meatballs

*These are bound to become a regular at your dinner table.*

| | |
|---|---|
| 1 pound ground beef | 1 to 1½ teaspoons pepper |
| ¼ cup coarsely chopped fresh parsley | ¾ cup dry bread crumbs |
| 2 eggs | 1½ teaspoons garlic powder |
| 1 teaspoon salt | ½ cup grated Parmesan cheese |

**P**reheat the oven to 350°F. In a large bowl, mix together all the ingredients. Form the mixture into meatballs, place on a cookie sheet that has been coated with nonstick vegetable spray, and bake for 25 to 30 minutes, or until done.

NOTE: Add to your favorite sauce and serve over spaghetti.

# italian turkey meatballs

12 meatballs

*Here's a lighter version of one of our all-time favorites.*
*I know, I know—ground turkey can be bland,*
*but not if it's seasoned well.*

| | |
|---|---|
| 1 pound ground turkey | 1 teaspoon fennel seed, crushed |
| 1 small onion, chopped | |
| 1 egg, beaten | ½ teaspoon garlic powder |
| ¼ cup dry bread crumbs | 1 teaspoon salt |
| 1 teaspoon dried thyme leaves | ½ teaspoon black pepper |
| | ¼ teaspoon cayenne pepper |

**P**reheat the oven to 350°F. In a large bowl, mix together all the ingredients. Form the mixture into meatballs, place on a cookie sheet that has been coated with nonstick vegetable spray, and bake for 20 minutes, or until no pink remains.

NOTE: Add to your favorite sauce and serve over spaghetti.

# golden baked macaroni

8 to 10 servings

*Here's another way to make pasta that'll make you happy
because it's so easy. And the best part is that it
will have everyone asking for seconds.*

1 pound elbow macaroni or
  other medium pasta shape

1 cup ricotta cheese

2 cups (8 ounces) shredded
  mozzarella cheese

2 cans (8 ounces each) tomato
  sauce

1 teaspoon salt

½ teaspoon pepper

¼ cup grated Parmesan cheese

Butter or margarine
  (optional)

**P**reheat the oven to 350°F. In a large pot of boiling salted water, cook the macaroni to desired doneness; drain. In a large bowl, combine the ricotta and mozzarella cheeses, tomato sauce, salt, and pepper. Add the macaroni to the mixture and toss lightly. Place in a 9" × 13" baking dish that has been coated with nonstick vegetable spray. Sprinkle with the Parmesan cheese and dot with butter. Bake, uncovered, for about 30 minutes, or until golden.

NOTE: This is great as is, but you might want to serve it topped with a chunky spaghetti sauce or maybe even some pesto sauce.

# turkey macaroni casserole

4 to 6 servings

*A whole Italian meal in one dish—the family will love it!*

| | |
|---|---|
| 1 pound ground turkey | ½ teaspoon black pepper |
| 1 medium-sized green bell pepper, chopped | ⅛ teaspoon garlic powder |
| 1 cup sliced onion rings | 8 ounces (2 cups) elbow macaroni |
| 1 can (15 ounces) tomato sauce | ½ cup milk |
| ½ teaspoon salt | 1 large egg, beaten |
| ½ teaspoon Italian seasoning | ½ to 1 cup (2 to 4 ounces) shredded mozzarella cheese |
| ½ teaspoon dried oregano | |

In a medium-sized skillet, combine the turkey, green pepper, and onion rings; cook until the turkey is no longer pink and green pepper is tender. Add the tomato sauce, salt, Italian seasoning, oregano, black pepper, and garlic powder. Bring the mixture to a boil, reduce the heat, and simmer for 20 minutes. Meanwhile, in a large pot of boiling water, cook the macaroni to desired doneness; drain. Preheat the oven to 350°F. Blend the milk and egg in a medium-sized bowl. Add the macaroni and meat mixture; mix well. Place the mixture in a greased 2-quart casserole, top with mozzarella cheese, and bake until heated through, about 20 minutes. Let stand for about 5 minutes for easier serving.

# chop suey pasta

about 6 servings

*Funny name? Well, it's not that it's Chinese-tasting . . . it's a mixture all thrown together, like chop suey.*

¾ pound (12 ounces) small pasta shape, like small shells or elbows

2 tablespoons vegetable oil

1 cup chopped celery

1 cup chopped green bell pepper

1 pound ground beef

1 can (10¾ ounces) condensed tomato soup

Salt to taste

Pepper to taste

2 cups (8 ounces) shredded Cheddar cheese, divided

**P**reheat the oven to 350°F. In a large pot of boiling salted water, cook the pasta to desired doneness; drain and place in a large bowl. Meanwhile, in a large skillet, heat the oil over medium-high heat; sauté the celery and green pepper until tender, then drain off the excess fat. Return the vegetables to the skillet and add the ground beef; cook the beef until no pink remains. Add the ground beef–vegetable mixture to the pasta. Gently stir in the tomato soup, add salt and pepper, then stir in 1 cup of the shredded Cheddar cheese. Place the mixture in a 2-quart casserole dish that has been coated with nonstick vegetable spray and top with the remaining 1 cup of Cheddar cheese. Bake for 30 minutes. Serve hot.

# quick macaroni casserole

about 6 servings

*A family favorite that's quick and so much more (like delicious, inexpensive, and so, so home-tasting).*

| | | | |
|---|---|---|---|
| 1 | tablespoon vegetable oil | 1 | teaspoon onion powder |
| 1 | pound ground beef | 1 | teaspoon garlic powder |
| ½ | pound elbow macaroni | 1 | teaspoon Italian seasoning |
| 2 | cups spaghetti sauce | ½ | teaspoon pepper |
| 2 | teaspoons salt | | |

**P**reheat the oven to 350°F. In a large skillet, heat the oil over medium-high heat; brown the beef, stirring to break it up, until no pink remains. Meanwhile, in a large pot of boiling salted water, cook the macaroni to desired doneness; drain and set aside in a large bowl. Lower the heat under the skillet, then add the spaghetti sauce, salt, onion powder, garlic powder, Italian seasoning, and pepper; mix well, then remove from the heat. Add to the macaroni and mix. Pour the mixture into a 2-quart casserole dish that has been coated with nonstick vegetable spray and bake for 1 hour, or until top is crispy golden.

# pasta and ground beef casserole

4 to 6 servings

*Nothing warms you up like a good, hearty casserole.*
*Great for a winter*
*meal or anytime you want to give your family a food "hug."*

½ pound elbows or shells
1 tablespoon vegetable oil
1 pound ground beef

2 cups (8 ounces) shredded Cheddar cheese
4 tablespoons chopped green olives
2 cups spaghetti sauce

**P**reheat the oven to 350°F. In a large pot of boiling salted water, cook the pasta to desired doneness; drain and set aside. In a large skillet, heat the oil over medium-high heat; brown the ground beef, then drain off the excess liquid. In a 2-quart casserole, layer half the pasta, half the beef, half the Cheddar cheese, half the olives, and half the spaghetti sauce. Repeat the layers. Cover and bake for about 1 hour, or until heated through.

# capellini with shrimp and herb sauce

about 4 servings

*I bet you think this sounds fancy. I bet they'll think this tastes
fancy, with its delicate lemon flavor. Well, that's the beauty
of it—sounds and tastes fancy but needs no fancy work!*

- 1 pound capellini (angel hair pasta)
- 3 tablespoons olive oil, plus extra for tossing
- 3 tablespoons butter
- 1 pound raw shrimp, shelled and deveined
- 2 garlic cloves, minced
- 1 teaspoon fresh lemon juice
- 1 teaspoon dried basil
- 1 tablespoon chopped fresh parsley
- 1 teaspoon dried oregano
- 1 tablespoon dried dillweed
- 2 cans (10½ ounces each) chicken broth
- Pepper to taste

**I**n a large pot of boiling salted water, cook the capellini until
just barely tender; drain, rinse, and place in a large bowl. Toss the
capellini with a little olive oil to keep it from sticking together.
Meanwhile, in a large skillet, heat the 3 tablespoons of olive oil
and melt the butter over medium heat; add the shrimp and garlic
and sauté until the shrimp just turns pink. Stir in the lemon juice,
basil, parsley, oregano, dillweed, and chicken broth; reduce the
heat and simmer until heated through. Pour the shrimp mixture
over the capellini and toss gently until the capellini is lightly
coated. Season with pepper and serve.

# seafood pasta

about 4 servings

*When you hear "seafood," you think expensive.*
*Not this one . . . and*
*you can even substitute imitation crabmeat for the salmon.*

1 pound capellini (angel hair pasta)

Melted butter for tossing

¾ pound bay scallops

¼ pound smoked salmon, cut into ½-inch pieces

2 garlic cloves, minced

1 cup half-and-half

1 cup milk

2 teaspoons dried dillweed

1 package (12 ounces) mushrooms, sliced

¼ cup grated Parmesan cheese

Salt to taste

Pepper to taste

In a large pot of boiling salted water, cook the capellini to desired doneness; drain, toss with melted butter, and place in a large bowl. Meanwhile, place the scallops, salmon, garlic, half-and-half, milk, dillweed, and mushrooms in a large saucepan and cook until moderately hot (do not boil). Reduce the heat and simmer until the scallops are cooked thoroughly (creamy white and no longer translucent). Pour the mixture over the capellini, add the grated Parmesan cheese, salt, and pepper, and toss well; serve.

# special day shrimp

3 to 4 servings

*If you want to cook something special for that special person,
here's an easy one that's filled with love and great taste!*

¼ cup vegetable oil

¼ cup chopped onion

2 teaspoons chopped fresh
garlic

⅛ teaspoon crushed red
pepper

¼ cup chopped parsley

½ teaspoon dried oregano

½ teaspoon dried basil

1 can (28 ounces) whole
tomatoes, undrained and
coarsely chopped

Dash of salt

1 to 1¼ pounds medium-sized
shrimp, cooked and peeled

In a large skillet, heat the oil over medium-high heat. Sauté the
onion, garlic, and red pepper until the onion is just transparent.
Add the parsley, oregano, basil, tomatoes and their juice, and salt;
stir thoroughly. Reduce the heat to medium and cook for 20
minutes, stirring occasionally. Add the shrimp, cover, and cook for
2 to 3 minutes more.

NOTE: Serve over linguine or your favorite pasta. And go ahead
and use chopped clams, scallops, or crabmeat instead of shrimp,
if you prefer.

# shortcut italian fisherman's spaghetti

### 6 to 8 servings

*Wow! It almost takes longer to say this one than it does to
make it. Well, it doesn't matter—it's so good that nobody
will be talking 'cause their mouths will be full
(and their smiles plentiful)!*

- 3 tablespoons olive oil, divided
- 1 cup chopped onion
- 3 garlic cloves, finely chopped
- 2 jars (26 to 28 ounces each) spaghetti sauce
- 2 cups sliced zucchini (about 1 medium-sized)
- 1 pound uncooked fresh (or thawed frozen) medium-sized shrimp, peeled and deveined
- ½ pound imitation crabmeat
- 1 pound spaghetti
- 2 tablespoons grated Parmesan cheese

In a large saucepan, heat 2 tablespoons of the oil over medium-high heat; cook the onion and garlic until tender. Add the spaghetti sauce and zucchini. Bring to a boil, reduce the heat, and simmer, uncovered, for 10 minutes. Add the shrimp and imitation crabmeat; cover and simmer for 8 minutes more, or until tender; stir. Meanwhile, in a large pot of boiling salted water, cook the spaghetti to desired doneness; drain and place in a large bowl. Toss the spaghetti with the remaining 1 tablespoon of olive oil and Parmesan cheese. Serve the sauce over the spaghetti.

# penne with tuna sauce

about 4 servings

*Come on, you know what to do with this one!*
*With a salad and some crusty bread,*
*you'll have a dinner your family will love.*
*It's like a romantic "fisherman's lunch" on the Italian coast.*

4 tablespoons olive oil

1 medium-sized onion, chopped

2 garlic cloves, crushed

6 anchovy fillets

1 can (28 ounces) whole tomatoes, broken up

2 cans (6½ ounces each) tuna

⅛ teaspoon salt

⅛ teaspoon pepper

1 pound penne or ziti

4 tablespoons chopped fresh parsley

2 tablespoons butter or margarine

In a large skillet, heat the oil over medium-high heat; add the onion and sauté until transparent, about 5 minutes. Add the garlic and continue to cook until the onion starts to brown. Add the anchovies, crushing them with a spoon. Add the tomatoes; reduce the heat and simmer, covered, for about 15 minutes. Drain the tuna and break into large flakes; add to the tomato sauce. Add the salt and pepper. Simmer, uncovered, for 5 minutes. The juices will evaporate and the sauce will thicken. Meanwhile, in a large pot of boiling salted water, cook the pasta to desired doneness; drain and place in a large serving bowl. Pour the sauce over the pasta. Add the parsley and butter and toss. Serve immediately.

# tuna linguine

4 servings

*Here's how you can put a complete and healthy meal
on the table when you've got very little time.
(But it's great anytime!)
It's like a pasta done Niçoise style . . . very fresh, very
Mediterranean, very chic—a sure applause-getter.*

| | |
|---|---|
| 1 can (6½ ounces) solid white tuna, packed in water, drained | ½ teaspoon garlic powder |
| | 1 teaspoon salt |
| 6 to 7 tablespoons olive oil | ¼ teaspoon pepper |
| 2 teaspoons lemon juice | ½ teaspoon dried dillweed |
| ½ cup chopped fresh parsley | 1 pound linguine |

In a large bowl, break the tuna into pieces and add the oil. Combine with the lemon juice, parsley, garlic powder, salt, pepper, and dillweed. In a large pot of boiling salted water, cook the linguine to desired doneness; drain. Add the linguine to the tuna mixture and toss to combine well. Serve immediately.

# macaroni tuna skillet

about 4 servings

*Here's a quick throw-together meal that can come
from your pantry and taste anything but!*

1 package (7¼ ounces)
macaroni and cheese
dinner mix

½ cup milk

2 tablespoons margarine

3 cans (6½ ounces each)
tuna, drained and broken
into chunks

1 can or jar (4 ounces) sliced
mushrooms, undrained

2 teaspoons dried parsley
flakes

½ teaspoon paprika

½ teaspoon prepared mustard

1 cup (½ pint) sour cream

2 tablespoons dry white wine

**C**ook the macaroni from the dinner mix according to the package directions; drain. In a large skillet, over medium heat, combine the cooked macaroni, the cheese from the dinner mix, milk, and margarine. Stir in the tuna, undrained mushrooms, parsley, paprika, and mustard. Simmer, uncovered, for 5 to 10 minutes, stirring occasionally. Stir in the sour cream and wine; heat through and serve.

# linguine with garlic and anchovies

4 servings

*Can't get enough of this! Anchovies aren't for everybody
but if you're willing to give them a try this way,
you'll love them like I do.*

| | |
|---|---|
| 1 pound linguine | ¼ teaspoon pepper |
| ½ cup olive oil | ½ cup chopped parsley |
| 4 garlic cloves, sliced | |
| 2 cans (2 ounces each) anchovy fillets with oil | |

In a large pot of boiling salted water, cook the linguine to desired doneness; drain, reserving 1 cup of pasta cooking water, and place in a large serving bowl. Meanwhile, in a large skillet, heat the olive oil over medium heat; add the garlic and sauté until lightly browned. Remove from the heat and allow to cool slightly to prevent splattering, then add the anchovies, breaking them up. Mix in the pepper, parsley, and reserved pasta cooking water. Return the skillet to the stove and heat through. Pour the mixture over the linguine, toss gently, and serve.

# seashore fettuccine

3 to 4 servings

*Great seafood taste! Why, if you try really hard,
you can even smell that fresh ocean air!*

1 pound fettuccine

½ cup (1 stick) butter or margarine

1 small onion, diced

12 ounces frozen broken shrimp, thawed

¼ teaspoon dried basil

⅛ teaspoon crushed red pepper

½ teaspoon salt

Pinch of black pepper

1 can (8 ounces) tomato sauce

1 container (8 ounces) heavy cream

½ cup grated Parmesan cheese

In a large pot of boiling salted water, cook the fettuccine to desired doneness; drain, place in a large bowl, and set aside. In a large skillet, melt the butter over medium heat; add the onion, shrimp, basil, red pepper, salt, and black pepper. Sauté for about 2 minutes, then add the tomato sauce and heavy cream; bring to a boil. Simmer until the sauce is creamy, about 3 minutes. Add the sauce and Parmesan cheese to the fettuccine; toss and serve.

NOTE: This even tastes great with imitation crabmeat or scallops. In fact, whatever fish or seafood is on sale or in the freezer will work.

# veal piazza

4 servings

*Eating at home will feel like dining at an Italian bistro
with this hearty taste of Italy.* Buon appetito!

½ cup all-purpose flour
½ teaspoon salt
½ teaspoon black pepper
1½ pounds veal chunks
¼ cup olive oil
2 garlic cloves, chopped
1 large onion, chopped
3 green bell peppers, cut into large chunks

1 can (10½ ounces) chicken broth
1 can (28 ounces) whole tomatoes, undrained
¼ cup red wine
½ teaspoon dried oregano
½ teaspoon dried basil
⅛ teaspoon crushed red pepper
1 teaspoon sugar
1 pound spaghetti

In a shallow dish, combine the flour with the salt and black pepper; dredge the veal chunks in the mixture. Heat the oil in a Dutch oven over medium heat. Add the coated veal and cook until light golden, about 10 minutes, stirring occasionally. Add the garlic, onion, and green peppers and cook for 5 minutes more, stirring occasionally. Add the chicken broth, tomatoes with juice, red wine, oregano, basil, red pepper, and sugar, reduce the heat, and simmer for 10 minutes more, stirring occasionally. Meanwhile, in a large pot of boiling salted water, cook the spaghetti to desired doneness; drain. Serve the veal mixture over the spaghetti.

# chicken and linguine with garlic sauce

4 servings

*Here's a whole meal that'll have 'em coming back for more . . . and more . . . and more.*
*You get the idea! Don't be fooled by the nine cloves of garlic. After they're cooked, they turn out to be full-flavored, smooth, and mild. You'll be the whiz of the table!*

| | |
|---|---|
| 1 pound linguine | 2 whole cooked chicken breasts, skinned, boned and coarsely chopped |
| ¾ cup olive oil | |
| 9 garlic cloves, chopped | ¾ cup chicken broth |
| ½ teaspoon crushed red pepper | ½ teaspoon dried thyme |
| ½ teaspoon salt | |

In a large pot of boiling salted water, cook the linguine to desired doneness; drain and place in a large serving bowl. Meanwhile, in a large saucepan, heat the olive oil over medium heat; add the garlic and sauté for 5 minutes. Cool slightly to prevent splattering, then stir in the red pepper and salt. Gradually stir in the chicken, chicken broth, and thyme. Reduce the heat and simmer until heated through. Toss with the linguine and serve.

# lemon linguine with chicken

### 2 to 3 servings

*You're gonna really enjoy this light pasta—no heavy sauce
here 'cause the lemon adds that fresh "sparkle."*

2   tablespoons butter or
    margarine

2   chicken breasts, split,
    skinned, and boned

2   cups chicken broth

1   cup water

2   tablespoons fresh lemon
    juice

½   teaspoon finely grated
    lemon peel

1   tablespoon honey

⅛   teaspoon dried rosemary

¼   teaspoon salt

¼   teaspoon freshly ground
    black pepper

½   pound linguine or other long
    pasta shape

Chopped fresh parsley, for
    garnish (optional)

In a large saucepan, melt the butter over medium heat; add the
chicken and brown it for 3 to 4 minutes on each side. Remove the
chicken from the saucepan. Add the remaining ingredients, except
the pasta and parsley, then bring to a boil and add the pasta.
Reduce the heat, cover, and simmer for 10 minutes, stirring occasionally. Meanwhile, cut the cooked chicken into 2-inch by ¼-inch
strips. Add to the mixture, cover, and simmer for 5 minutes; stir.
Garnish with parsley and serve immediately.

# turkey fettuccine

2 to 3 servings

*You'll love this light variation of the traditional fettuccine dish.*
*And I don't know about you, but I'm always happy to find*
*a new way to enjoy turkey.*

½ pound fettuccine

3 tablespoons butter or
margarine

3 tablespoons all-purpose
flour

1 cup milk

1 cup chicken broth

¼ cup grated Parmesan cheese

¼ teaspoon salt

Dash of ground white
pepper

2 cups chopped skinless
turkey breast (about 10
ounces)

1 jar or can (4 ounces) sliced
mushrooms, drained

¼ cup chopped fresh parsley

In a large pot of boiling salted water, cook the fettuccine to desired doneness; drain, then place in a large bowl. Meanwhile, in a medium-sized saucepan, melt the butter over low heat. Stir in the flour and cook, stirring, for 1 to 2 minutes. Raise the heat to medium and gradually stir in the milk and broth. Continue to cook, stirring, until the sauce is thickened. Add the Parmesan cheese, salt, pepper, turkey, and mushrooms and continue to cook, stirring occasionally, until the turkey is hot. Mix in the parsley. Serve the turkey-mushroom mixture over the fettuccine.

# hamburger stroganoff

4 to 6 servings

*I know this sounds fancy and complicated, but take a look
to see how really easy it is.
Delicious, too, but you don't just have to take
my word for it . . . try it! Truly European, truly fulfilling.*

¼ cup (½ stick) margarine

1 pound ground beef

1 medium-sized onion, chopped (about ½ cup)

2 tablespoons all-purpose flour

1 teaspoon garlic powder

¼ teaspoon pepper

1 can (8 ounces) mushroom stems and pieces, drained

1 can (10½ ounces) cream of chicken soup

½ pound egg noodles

1 cup (½ pint) low-fat sour cream

**I**n a large skillet, melt the margarine over medium heat; cook the ground beef and onion until the meat is browned and onion is tender, stirring occasionally. Stir in the flour, garlic powder, pepper, and mushrooms. Cook for 5 minutes, stirring constantly. Reduce the heat to low and stir in the soup; simmer, uncovered, for 10 minutes, stirring occasionally. Meanwhile, in a large pot of boiling salted water, cook the noodles to desired doneness; drain. Remove the meat mixture from the heat and stir in the sour cream. Serve over the hot noodles.

NOTE: For a lower-fat stroganoff, substitute ground turkey for the ground beef and plain nonfat yogurt for the sour cream, and replace the soup with a low-fat cream of chicken soup. To "spice up" either version, add 1 teaspoon crushed dried thyme, 1 teaspoon crushed dried sage, and 1 teaspoon paprika when you add the garlic.

# sausage dinner

4 to 6 servings

*Here's homemade great taste but without all the fuss—*
*'cause it's all done in one pan! And the*
*sausage gives it so much full flavor.*

1 pound hot or sweet Italian sausage, crumbled

1 cup finely chopped onion

1 cup finely chopped green bell pepper

1 can (14½ ounces) whole tomatoes

1 cup sour cream

1 cup water

1 tablespoon sugar

2 teaspoons salt

1 teaspoon chili powder

½ pound (½ of a 16-ounce package) narrow or medium egg noodles

In a large skillet, combine the sausage, onion, and green pepper. Cook over medium heat until the sausage is brown and onion is tender; drain off the pan drippings. In a medium-sized bowl, combine the tomatoes, sour cream, water, sugar, salt, and chili powder; stir into the sausage mixture. Gently stir in the noodles. Cover and simmer for about 30 minutes or until the noodles are tender, stirring occasionally.

# tex-mex chili 'n' pasta

about 4 servings

*Here's a great way to combine some favorites—*
*Tex-Mex and Italian—*
*and, boy, do they ever work well together!*

| | | | |
|---|---|---|---|
| 2 | tablespoons vegetable oil | ½ | teaspoon cayenne pepper |
| 1½ | pounds stew beef, diced into ¼-inch chunks | ½ | teaspoon salt |
| 3 | garlic cloves, minced | 1 | can (14½ ounces) whole tomatoes |
| 2 | tablespoons chili powder | 3 | cups water |
| 1 | tablespoon ground cumin | 1 | jar (28 ounces) spaghetti sauce |
| | | ¾ | pound twist or elbow macaroni |

In a large skillet, heat the oil over medium-high heat; add the stew beef and garlic and brown lightly. Add the chili powder, cumin, cayenne pepper, and salt and stir to coat the beef. Add the tomatoes and water. Bring to a boil, then reduce the heat, cover, and simmer for 1½ hours, stirring occasionally. Add the spaghetti sauce, then continue to cook, uncovered, for 10 to 15 minutes, stirring occasionally, until heated through. Meanwhile, in a large pot of boiling salted water, cook the pasta to desired doneness; drain and place in a large bowl. Spoon the beef mixture over the hot pasta and serve.

NOTE: Why not try topping this with grated sharp cheese, chopped onions, or chopped jalapeño peppers?

# mostaccioli and sausage

4 to 6 servings

*Authentic Italian food without all the authentic work—*
*sounds good, doesn't it? (It is!)*

1½ pounds hot or sweet
Italian sausage links,
sliced about 1-inch thick

1 cup chopped onion

¾ cup chopped green bell
pepper

2 jars (26 to 28 ounces each)
spaghetti sauce

½ cup grated Parmesan cheese

1 pound mostaccioli

2 tablespoons olive oil

**B**rown the sausage in a large saucepan over medium-high heat; drain off the fat. Add the onion and green pepper; cook, stirring, until tender. Add the spaghetti sauce and Parmesan cheese. Bring to a boil; reduce the heat, cover, and simmer for 15 minutes, stirring occasionally. Meanwhile, in a large pot of boiling salted water, cook the mostaccioli to desired doneness; drain and place in a large bowl. Toss the hot mostaccioli with the olive oil; serve with the sauce.

NOTE: Sure, you can use another kind of pasta other than mostaccioli (mustache-shaped)—like penne, ziti, or shells. Just change the name as you change the shape (or they'll call you a "fibber"!).

# spaghetti with cauliflower and broccoli

3 to 4 servings

*Here's a way to eat light and healthy*
*without giving up delicious.*

¼ cup olive oil

4 garlic cloves, crushed

2 teaspoons Italian seasoning

1 package (16 ounces) frozen cauliflower and broccoli, thawed

1 teaspoon salt

1 teaspoon pepper

2 cups tomato purée

½ cup chopped fresh parsley

1 pound spaghetti

1½ cups grated Parmesan cheese

In a deep skillet, heat the olive oil. Add the garlic and Italian seasoning; sauté for about 1 minute. Add the cauliflower and broccoli, sprinkle with salt and pepper, and sauté until the cauliflower is tender, about 8 to 10 minutes. Then add the tomato purée and chopped parsley. Mix lightly, lower the heat to simmer, and cook for 15 minutes. Meanwhile, in a large pot of boiling salted water, cook the spaghetti to desired doneness; drain and place on a serving platter. Pour the cauliflower-broccoli mixture over the spaghetti, top with the Parmesan cheese, toss to mix, and serve immediately.

# tricolor pasta

### 4 to 6 servings

*Whether you use this as an appetizer or as a main course,
you'll be sure to hear "It's so colorful!" followed
quickly by "And it tastes as good as it looks!!"*

¼ cup plus 1 tablespoon olive oil, divided

¼ cup finely chopped onion

1 small garlic clove, crushed

2 cans (14½ ounces each) whole tomatoes with juice, broken up, or 3 cups peeled and chopped fresh tomatoes

Salt to taste

Freshly ground black pepper to taste

1 pound penne or other tubular pasta shape

½ cup chopped fresh basil leaves

Grated Parmesan cheese, for sprinkling (optional)

In a large skillet, heat the ¼ cup of olive oil over medium heat; add the onion and sauté until tender (do not brown). Add the garlic and sauté for 1 minute. Stir in the tomatoes; reduce the heat to medium low and simmer, stirring occasionally, until the sauce is slightly thickened, about 25 minutes. Add the salt and pepper to taste. In a large pot of boiling salted water, cook the pasta to desired doneness; drain well and place in a large bowl. Stir the 1 tablespoon of olive oil into the sauce, then pour the sauce over the pasta. Add the basil and toss to blend. Sprinkle with Parmesan cheese if desired, and serve.

# pasta and spinach

4 to 6 servings

*This is kind of like a pasta pudding—the taste is there but the work isn't. And it just gets better with age, so make it in advance, when you have more time.*

1 pound short tubular pasta shape, like ziti or rigatoni

SAUCE

⅔ cup grated Parmesan cheese

2 packages (10 ounces each) frozen chopped spinach, thawed and drained well

1 container (15 ounces) ricotta cheese

3 large eggs, beaten

⅓ cup chopped fresh parsley

2 teaspoons salt

2 teaspoons pepper

1 jar (28 to 32 ounces) spaghetti sauce

2 tablespoons grated Parmesan cheese

**P**reheat the oven to 375°F. In a large pot of boiling salted water, cook the pasta until just barely tender. Meanwhile, in a large bowl, combine the sauce ingredients; mix well. Drain the pasta, toss it with the sauce, and turn it into a greased 9" × 13" baking pan. Sprinkle the 2 tablespoons of Parmesan cheese over the top and bake for 25 to 30 minutes, or until bubbly and lightly browned.

NOTE: You can vary this in so many ways—by adding sausage, some fennel seed, a shake of oregano or garlic powder—whatever you like.

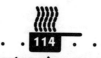

# garden ravioli

3 to 4 servings

*Packaged foods like ravioli can make meal preparation much easier. They're sensible, and you don't have to give up great taste, either. This proves it.*

24 large frozen cheese ravioli

¼ cup (½ stick) butter, melted

1 garlic clove, finely chopped

¼ cup chopped fresh parsley

¼ cup grated Parmesan cheese

¼ cup olive oil

3 to 4 tablespoons water

1 teaspoon dried basil

1 teaspoon dried oregano

¼ teaspoon salt

In a large pot of boiling salted water, cook the ravioli to desired doneness, about 10 minutes. Meanwhile, in a large bowl, combine all the remaining ingredients. Drain the ravioli quickly, add to the mixture, toss gently, and serve immediately.

# anthony's gnocchi

4 to 5 servings

*Never knew potato dumplings could be this good.*
*Thanks, Anthony.*

2 bags (1 pound each) frozen gnocchi (potato dumplings)

¼ cup olive oil

1 medium-sized onion, finely chopped

5 to 6 garlic cloves, minced

1 bag (3 ounces) sun-dried tomatoes, blanched, drained, and slivered

½ cup chopped stuffed green olives

½ cup dry sherry

1 cup heavy cream

**P**repare the gnocchi according to the package directions; drain, rinse with hot water, drain again, place in a large bowl, and set aside. Meanwhile, in a large skillet, heat the oil over medium-high heat; sauté the onion and garlic lightly, about 5 minutes. Add the sun-dried tomatoes and olives to the skillet and mix, then add the sherry. Mix again, bring to a boil, reduce the heat, and simmer for 15 minutes. Add the heavy cream, stir, then simmer until heated through. Mix with the gnocchi and serve.

# chinese noodles

4 to 6 servings

*This is a real treat as is, but some leftover
grilled chicken cut into bite-sized pieces
can make it into a whole meal.*

| | |
|---|---|
| 1 pound spaghetti | ½ teaspoon garlic powder |
| 2 tablespoons vegetable oil | ¼ cup soy sauce |
| 2 tablespoons hoisin sauce | ¼ teaspoon salt |
| ½ cup chopped scallion | ¼ teaspoon pepper |

In a large pot of boiling salted water, cook the spaghetti to desired doneness; drain. Place the spaghetti in a large bowl and mix with the vegetable oil. In a medium-sized bowl, mix together the remaining ingredients; add them to the spaghetti and serve.

# capellini with light sauce

about 4 servings

*Simple, quick, fresh . . . Just perfect when you want to feel
satisfied and summertime light at the same time.*

1 pound capellini (angel hair
  pasta) or other long, thin
  pasta shape

4 tablespoons vegetable oil

1 tablespoon minced garlic

5 cups diced fresh tomatoes

½ teaspoon dried basil

Salt to taste

Freshly ground black pepper
  to taste

¾ cup chicken broth

5 tablespoons grated
  Parmesan cheese, for
  tossing

In a large pot of boiling salted water, cook the pasta to desired
doneness; drain and place in a large bowl. Meanwhile, in a large
skillet, heat the oil to medium-high heat; add the garlic and cook
for 1 minute. Add the tomatoes, basil, salt, and pepper; cook for 3
minutes more. Add the chicken broth and stir until heated through.
Pour the mixture over the hot pasta, toss with Parmesan cheese,
and serve immediately.

# creamy blue cheese pasta

about 4 servings

*Red sauces, white sauces, garlic, and oil—I love 'em all,*
*but sometimes I just want something a little different*
*with my pasta. And for cheese lovers??? Wow!!!*

| | | | |
|---|---|---|---|
| 1 | pound spaghetti | ¾ | cup minced scallion |
| 4 | tablespoons butter | 2 | tablespoons fresh lemon juice |
| ½ | cup blue cheese (about 3 ounces), crumbled | | |
| ¾ | cup chicken broth | ½ | teaspoon salt |
| 1½ | cups sliced mushrooms | ¼ | teaspoon pepper |
| | | ¼ | cup grated Parmesan cheese |

In a large pot of boiling salted water, cook the spaghetti to desired doneness; drain and place in a large bowl. Meanwhile, in a large skillet over medium heat, place the butter, blue cheese, and chicken broth. Stir until the mixture has thickened slightly (enough to coat the back of a spoon), about 5 minutes. Add the mushrooms, scallion, lemon juice, salt, and pepper and cook for 5 minutes more. Pour the mixture over the spaghetti and toss to blend thoroughly. Sprinkle with the Parmesan cheese and serve.

# family favorites

# shrimp macaroni salad

6 to 8 servings

*Seafood and pasta—two favorites in one dish!*
*And in a snap!*

½ pound elbow macaroni or
   shells

8 ounces cooked shrimp,
   drained and coarsely
   chopped

1 medium tomato, diced

1 small onion, diced

2 large hard-boiled eggs, diced

1 tablespoon seafood
   seasoning

¼ teaspoon garlic salt

¾ cup mayonnaise

Salt to taste

Pepper to taste

In a large pot of boiling water, cook the pasta to desired doneness; drain. In a large bowl, toss the pasta with the remaining ingredients. Cover; chill before serving.

# antipasto salad with white bean dressing

6 to 8 servings
(about 1 cup dressing)

*This is no longer reserved for fancy Italian restaurants.*
*Now you can enjoy it at home*
*and no one will guess how simple it was to*
*throw together. That's okay, let 'em think you fussed.*

½ pound rainbow rotini

1 teaspoon dried oregano

1 head lettuce, separated into leaves

1 can (14 ounces) artichoke hearts, drained and cut into quarters

2 cans (6½ ounces each) tuna in water, drained

1 can (6 ounces) pitted ripe olives, drained

⅔ cup (about ½ of a 15-ounce can) great Northern beans, rinsed and drained

2 small tomatoes, cut into wedges

1 medium cucumber, peeled and sliced

1 small red onion, peeled and sliced

4 ounces feta cheese, cut into cubes or crumbled

WHITE BEAN DRESSING

⅔ cup (½ of a 15-ounce can) great Northern beans, rinsed and drained

3 tablespoons olive or vegetable oil

1 tablespoon Dijon-style mustard

3 tablespoons milk or as needed

2 tablespoons lemon juice

Salt to taste

White pepper to taste

In a medium-sized pot of boiling salted water, cook the rotini to desired doneness; drain, cool, and return to the pot. Toss the rotini with the oregano. On a large serving platter, make a bed of lettuce; arrange the rotini, artichoke hearts, tuna, olives, beans, tomatoes, cucumber, and onion slices attractively. Distribute feta

**family favorites**

cheese over everything. In a food processor or blender, make the dressing by processing the beans, oil, and mustard until smooth; add enough milk to make the desired dressing consistency. Season the bean mixture with the lemon juice, salt, and pepper and serve over the antipasto salad.

# fettuccine alfredo primavera

4 servings

*Another all-time favorite made simple, and more*
*"today style"—you'll love it!*

SAUCE

1 pint heavy cream

4 ounces (1 stick) butter

6 ounces (6 wedges) soft
processed Gruyère cheese,
like Laughing Cow®, Bon
Bel®, or Tiger Brand®

1 pound fettuccine

1 package (16 ounces) frozen
cauliflower, broccoli, and
carrot combination, thawed
and blanched

½ cup grated Parmesan cheese

In a medium-sized saucepan or in a double boiler, combine all
the sauce ingredients. Cook over a low heat until everything is
melted and the sauce is velvety smooth, about 20 minutes. Meanwhile, in a large pot of boiling salted water, cook the fettuccine to
desired doneness; drain and place in a large bowl. Mix in the vegetables and sauce, and sprinkle with the Parmesan cheese. Serve
immediately.

NOTE: You may want to try a lower-fat version of this recipe (page
150), or maybe make it with Tomato Cream Sauce (page 149).

# marinara sauce

about 4 cups
(enough for 1 to 2 pounds of pasta)

*Everybody needs a good, basic marinara sauce recipe.*
*Here's one that I use all the time,*
*'cause it's so super-easy and super-"real."*

¼ cup olive oil

4 garlic cloves, coarsely chopped

1 can (28 ounces) crushed tomatoes

1 cup water

¾ cup chopped fresh parsley

1 teaspoon salt

1 teaspoon pepper

1 teaspoon dried oregano

1 teaspoon garlic powder

In a large skillet, heat the olive oil over medium-high heat; add the garlic and sauté until golden. Allow to cool slightly to avoid splattering, then add the tomatoes and water and bring to a rapid boil. Add the parsley, salt, pepper, oregano, and garlic powder. Lower the heat to medium and cook for 10 minutes more, stirring occasionally.

NOTE: Serve over spaghetti and add a sprinkle of Parmesan cheese, if you like, or, you can try one of these variations:

Fra Diavolo: When adding the other seasonings, add ⅛ to ¼ teaspoon crushed red pepper.

Seafood Marinara: After the basic sauce is cooked, add shrimp, clams, scallops, or any combination of them (about 18 to 24 pieces of seafood) and cook for about 10 minutes more, or until the seafood is cooked thoroughly.

Chicken Marinara: After the basic sauce is cooked, add 2 boneless, skinless, cooked chicken breasts that have been cut into strips, allowing to heat through.

# sunday pranzo sauce with meatballs

about 10 cups

*This is authentic Italian. It was served every
Sunday afternoon, without fail,
at my friend's house. (Oh, how I looked
forward to being invited over!)*

MEATBALLS

| | |
|---|---|
| 1 | pound ground beef |
| ¼ | cup coarsely chopped fresh parsley |
| 2 | large eggs |
| 1 | teaspoon salt |
| 1 to 1½ | teaspoons pepper |
| ¾ | cup dry bread crumbs |
| 1½ | teaspoons garlic powder |
| ½ | cup grated Parmesan cheese |

| | |
|---|---|
| 1½ | cups olive oil |
| 4 | garlic cloves, coarsely chopped |
| 1 | pound Italian sausage links |
| 3 | cans (28 ounces each) crushed tomatoes |
| 42 | ounces water (fill a crushed tomato can 1½ times) |
| ½ | cup chopped fresh parsley |
| 1 | tablespoon pepper |
| 2 | teaspoons garlic powder |
| 2 | teaspoons salt |
| 1 | teaspoon dried oregano |

In a large bowl, mix together all the meatball ingredients. Form the mixture into about 12 medium-sized meatballs and set aside. In a large pot, heat the olive oil over medium heat; sauté the garlic, sausage, and meatballs and continue cooking until the meat is golden brown, firm, and cooked through, about 20 minutes. Remove the cooked meat from pot and set aside. Remove the pot from the stove and allow to cool slightly to avoid splattering, then add the remaining ingredients; mix thoroughly. Simmer over a low heat for 20 minutes, stirring occasionally. Return the meat to the pot and simmer for 1 to 2 hours more, stirring occasionally.

NOTE: Serve over spaghetti or your favorite pasta.

family favorites

# better baked ziti

about 8 servings

*Everyone tells me that this is the best baked ziti they've ever had. I have to agree—it works every time.*

½ pound ziti

1 container (15 ounces) ricotta cheese

3 cups (12 ounces) shredded mozzarella cheese, divided

3 cups spaghetti sauce, divided

½ cup grated Parmesan cheese

**P**reheat the oven to 350°F. In a large pot of boiling salted water, cook the ziti until just barely tender; drain and place in a large bowl. Mix the ricotta cheese and half of the mozzarella cheese with the ziti. Grease a 9" × 13" baking pan; cover the bottom of pan with half the spaghetti sauce. Spoon the ziti mixture into the pan; cover with the remaining spaghetti sauce. Sprinkle with the Parmesan cheese and top with the remaining mozzarella cheese. Bake for 20 to 30 minutes, or until cheese melts and is lightly golden.

NOTE: I especially like the new hearty-style prepared spaghetti sauces with this, and when I don't have ziti on hand, I simply substitute other shapes.

# spaghetti bolognese

4 to 6 servings

*One of the all-time favorite one-dish suppers is spaghetti with meat sauce. Here's a way to make it with a thick sauce that always sticks to the spaghetti.*

1 pound ground beef, turkey, or pork

1 cup chopped onion

1 cup shredded carrots

1 garlic clove, crushed

1 beef bouillon cube

1 teaspoon dried basil

1 teaspoon dried oregano

1 teaspoon sugar

2 cans (15 ounces each) tomato sauce

1 pound regular or thin spaghetti

In a large skillet, brown the ground beef over medium-high heat; drain off the fat. Add the onion, carrots, and garlic. Cook, stirring, for about 5 minutes, or until the onion is tender. Add the remaining ingredients except the spaghetti. Cover, reduce the heat, and simmer for 20 minutes, stirring occasionally. Meanwhile, in a large pot of boiling salted water, cook the spaghetti to desired doneness. Drain, place in a serving bowl, and pour the sauce over it.

# linguine with white clam sauce

4 servings

*There are so many good ways to enjoy pasta—here's
an old-fashioned classic made easy!*

½ cup olive oil

2 to 3 garlic cloves, minced

2 cans (6½ ounces each)
minced clams with juice

½ cup clam juice

½ cup chopped fresh parsley

½ teaspoon dried oregano

½ teaspoon dried basil

¼ to ½ teaspoon salt

⅛ teaspoon crushed red
pepper

¼ teaspoon black pepper

1 pound linguine

In a large skillet, heat the olive oil over medium heat; sauté the
garlic for about 5 minutes, or until golden. Add the minced clams,
clam juice, parsley, oregano, basil, salt, and red and black pepper.
Simmer, stirring occasionally, for 10 minutes. Meanwhile, in a large
pot of boiling water, cook the linguine to desired doneness; drain.
Serve the clam sauce over the linguine.

# noodle pudding
about 15 servings

*Love . . . it's the secret ingredient in here. This is an old family favorite, and when they taste yours, they'll know you added that "something" special.*

½ pound wide egg noodles

1 container (16 ounces) sour cream

1 cup cottage cheese (½ of a 16-ounce container)

6 large eggs, lightly beaten

1 cup sugar

1 teaspoon salt

1 cup fruit cocktail (½ of a 16-ounce can)

Ground cinnamon, for topping

**P**reheat the oven to 400°F. In a large pot of boiling water, cook the noodles to desired doneness; drain. Meanwhile, in a large bowl, combine the sour cream, cottage cheese, eggs, sugar, and salt. Fold in the fruit cocktail, then add the noodles and mix gently. Transfer the mixture to a 9" × 13" baking pan that has been coated with nonstick vegetable spray. Sprinkle with a little cinnamon, then bake for 30 minutes. Lower the oven heat to 325°F. and bake for another 15 to 20 minutes, or until golden and set. Let cool for 10 minutes before serving.

NOTE: This is great rewarmed, too!

# apple lasagna

## 12 to 15 servings

*I know! I know! Sounds strange, doesn't it? Well, I sure would*
*be surprised if this doesn't become a favorite snack or dessert*
*with your family—it sure did with mine. Just think about a*
*noodle pudding that'll be the conversation piece of*
*the table—and you'll be the "expert"!*

8 lasagna noodles

2 cans (21 ounces each) apple
  pie filling

### CHEESE FILLING

2 cups (8 ounces) shredded
  Cheddar cheese

1 cup ricotta cheese

1 large egg, beaten

¼ cup granulated sugar

### TOPPING

6 tablespoons all-purpose
  flour

½ teaspoon ground cinnamon

3 tablespoons margarine

6 tablespoons light or dark
  brown sugar

¼ cup quick oats

Dash of ground nutmeg

### SOUR CREAM GARNISH
(optional)

1 cup (½ pint) sour cream

⅓ cup light or dark brown
  sugar

**P**reheat the oven to 350°F. In a large pot of boiling salted water, cook the noodles to desired doneness; drain and set aside. Spread 1 can of the apple pie filling in a greased 9" × 13" baking pan, slicing any extra-thick apples. Layer 4 noodles over the apples. In a large bowl, mix together the cheese filling ingredients; spread them evenly over the noodles and top with the remaining 4 noodles. Spoon the remaining can of apple pie filling over noodles. In a small bowl, crumble together the topping ingredients. Sprinkle

(continued)

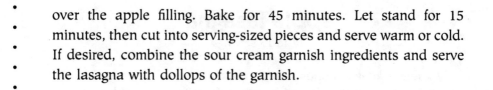

over the apple filling. Bake for 45 minutes. Let stand for 15 minutes, then cut into serving-sized pieces and serve warm or cold. If desired, combine the sour cream garnish ingredients and serve the lasagna with dollops of the garnish.

# pasta sauces

# quick meat sauce

about 9 cups
(enough for 1 to 2 pounds of pasta)

*Here's one that no pasta lover should be without—it's as good as the old-fashioned sauce that Grandma used to make, but, like the name says, it's quick!*

2 tablespoons vegetable oil

2 medium-sized onions, chopped

1 medium-sized green bell pepper, chopped

1 pound bulk Italian sausage, broken up

1 pound ground beef, broken up

1 can (28 ounces) whole tomatoes, undrained, broken up

1 can (15 ounces) tomato sauce

1 can (6 ounces) tomato paste

½ cup water

½ cup chopped fresh or ¼ cup dried parsley

2 teaspoons Italian seasoning

1½ teaspoons salt

1 teaspoon sugar

1 teaspoon garlic powder

¼ teaspoon freshly ground black pepper

**I**n a large skillet or saucepan, heat the oil over medium-high heat; sauté the onions and green pepper for 5 minutes. Add the sausage and ground beef and cook until the meat is no longer pink and the vegetables are tender, about 8 minutes more; drain. Stir in the remaining ingredients. Bring to a boil, then reduce the heat and simmer for 30 minutes, stirring occasionally.

NOTE: Serve over spaghetti or your favorite pasta.

# farm-style pasta sauce

about 4 cups
(enough for 1 pound of pasta)

*A really full-flavored sauce that'll make any pasta taste great.*

¼ cup olive oil

2 garlic cloves, finely minced

1 can (15 ounces) crushed
tomatoes

1 cup pitted ripe olives,
halved

½ cup loosely packed basil
leaves, coarsely chopped, or
1 heaping tablespoon dried
basil

¼ teaspoon salt

1 teaspoon pepper

½ teaspoon sugar

½ cup chicken broth

1 can (14½ ounces) whole
tomatoes, drained and
coarsely broken

**I**n a large skillet, heat the olive oil over medium heat; add the garlic and sauté for about 1 minute, or until light golden. Add the crushed tomatoes, olives, basil, salt, and pepper; cook for about 2 minutes more, stirring occasionally. Add the sugar, chicken broth, and broken tomatoes and cook for 2 minutes more, stirring occasionally.

NOTE: Serve over spaghetti or your favorite pasta, and, if you'd like, sprinkle with a little Parmesan cheese.

# zucchini and fresh tomato sauce

4 to 6 servings

(about 6 cups)

*"Summer in a saucepan" because of all the fresh veggies—and the best part is that you can enjoy it all year 'round!*

3 tablespoons vegetable oil

3 garlic cloves, finely chopped

1 medium-sized onion, coarsely chopped

3 tomatoes, seeded and coarsely chopped

3 medium-sized zucchini, sliced into ¼" rounds

2 teaspoons salt

½ teaspoon pepper

1 teaspoon dried oregano

1 teaspoon dried basil

In a large saucepan, heat the oil; sauté the garlic and onion until the onion becomes transparent. Add the tomatoes and continue cooking until the tomatoes soften, about 5 to 10 minutes. Add the remaining ingredients and simmer over a low heat for 15 to 20 minutes more, stirring occasionally.

NOTE: Serve over 1 pound of spaghetti or your favorite pasta sprinkled with Parmesan cheese—it's a whole meal. This is so easy, and it tastes even fresher with fresh basil and parsley if you have them handy!

# sicilian olive sauce

about 4 cups

(enough for 1 pound of pasta)

*A rich Mediterranean taste that's a meal in itself. Count me in!*

- 2 cups prepared spaghetti sauce
- 1 jar (6 ounces) red roasted peppers, drained and coarsely chopped
- 1 jar (6 ounces) marinated artichoke hearts
- 1 can (6 ounces) pitted ripe olives, drained
- 2 cooked boneless and skinless chicken breasts, chunked
- 1 can (8 ounces) tomato sauce

**P**lace all the ingredients in a saucepan and heat until warmed through.

NOTE: Serve over spaghetti or linguine.

# country-style sauce

about 8 cups
(enough for about 2 pounds of pasta)

*Here's a fresh, chunky sauce that's sure to become a family
favorite. (It's great 'cause it works with
almost any chunky veggie!)*

½ cup olive oil

1 medium-sized eggplant,
diced

1 medium-sized onion, diced

2 garlic cloves, crushed

1 teaspoon dried rosemary,
crushed

¼ cup water

1 tablespoon lemon juice

2 jars (28 ounces each)
spaghetti sauce

In a large pot, heat the olive oil over medium-high heat; sauté the eggplant, onion, and garlic for about 5 minutes, or until just softened. Add the rosemary, water, lemon juice, and spaghetti sauce. Heat to boiling, reduce the heat, and simmer for about 10 minutes.

NOTE: Serve over spaghetti or your favorite pasta. Sometimes I add in a chopped green pepper, some broccoli, green beans, frozen peas, or a combination! And, if I have time, I also mix in ½ pound of browned ground meat to make it a rich meat sauce.

# fresh tomato sauce

about 4 cups

*This really gets my mouth watering! And when I get the urge
to have it, I can whip it up in no time,
'cause there's no cooking.*

½ cup vegetable oil

2 garlic cloves, peeled

½ teaspoon salt

1 teaspoon dried oregano

1 tablespoon dried basil or 2 tablespoons chopped fresh basil

1 teaspoon sugar

1 tablespoon wine vinegar

½ teaspoon hot pepper sauce

½ teaspoon grated Parmesan cheese

4 ripe tomatoes, seeded and diced

¼ cup chopped scallion

**P**lace the oil, garlic, salt, oregano, basil, sugar, vinegar, hot pepper sauce, and Parmesan cheese in a blender; purée until smooth. Pour the purée into a large bowl, then mix in the diced tomatoes and scallion. Serve at room temperature.

NOTE: Serve over spaghetti or your favorite pasta. And go ahead—add whatever seasonings you want to make it your own.

# light tomato wine sauce

about 4 cups

*Here's the "great light way" to enjoy your favorite pasta!*

1 tablespoon vegetable oil

1 medium-sized onion, chopped

2 garlic cloves, minced

6 medium-sized tomatoes, seeded and cut up

1 teaspoon sugar

½ teaspoon dried basil

¼ cup red wine

¼ cup beef broth

1 tablespoon wine vinegar

1 teaspoon salt

1 teaspoon pepper

In a large skillet, heat the oil over medium-high heat; sauté the onion and garlic until the onion is tender. Add the remaining ingredients to the skillet, stirring to blend, reduce the heat, and simmer for 15 to 20 minutes, or until the mixture is heated through (do not overcook).

NOTE: Serve over spaghetti or your favorite pasta.

# presto pasta sauce

about 3½ cups
(enough for 1 pound of pasta)

*Anchovies? Olives? Capers? Yup, put 'em together and you get*
*a delicious, rich pasta sauce that'll have them*
*asking for more. You'll see!!*

| | |
|---|---|
| ¼ cup olive oil | 2 tablespoons capers, drained |
| 1 garlic clove, finely minced | 1 can (28 ounces) crushed tomatoes |
| 6 anchovy fillets, coarsely chopped | 1 teaspoon dried oregano |
| ½ cup sliced black olives | ¼ teaspoon salt |
| | ¼ teaspoon pepper |

In a medium-sized saucepan, heat the oil over medium-high heat; add the garlic and sauté until golden (do not brown). Add the remaining ingredients. Cook, uncovered, until the mixture is heated through and has reduced slightly, about 10 minutes.

NOTE: To serve, toss with hot spaghetti and sprinkle with Parmesan cheese.

# old-fashioned, almost-basic tomato sauce

about 12 cups

*There are lots of different pasta sauces, but this one
is pure simplicity. It's a must for any pasta lover.*

- 1 medium-sized onion, peeled and quartered
- 3 celery stalks, cut into chunks
- 3 carrots, peeled and cut into chunks
- ¼ cup water
- 1 cup olive oil
- 4 cans (28 ounces each) crushed tomatoes
- ½ teaspoon dried basil
- ¼ cup chopped fresh parsley
- 3 garlic cloves, chopped
- ⅛ teaspoon crushed red pepper
- ½ cup dry red wine
- 2 teaspoons salt
- ½ teaspoon black pepper
- ¼ cup sugar
- 2 teaspoons garlic powder

In a blender or food processor, purée the onion, celery, and carrots; add the water and mix. In a large saucepan, combine the olive oil and vegetable purée and cook over medium heat; simmer for 5 to 8 minutes. Add the remaining ingredients; bring to a boil, then reduce the heat and simmer for about 1½ hours, stirring frequently.

NOTE: Serve over your favorite pasta.

# garlic tomato sauce

4 servings
(about 4 cups)

*Here's a sauce recipe you'll want to keep on hand
for another delicious way to serve pasta,
for that "once in a while" change.*

1½ cups hot water

2 tablespoons olive oil

1 tablespoon finely chopped green bell pepper

1 teaspoon dried basil

1 tablespoon instant chicken bouillon granules

4 garlic cloves

½ teaspoon ground black pepper

2 cups spaghetti sauce

In a blender, combine all the ingredients except the spaghetti sauce; process until smooth. In a saucepan, warm the spaghetti sauce, add the blended mixture, and heat through, stirring occasionally.

NOTE: Serve over capellini (angel hair) or your favorite pasta.

**pasta sauces**

# tomato-dill cream sauce

about 4 cups
(enough for 1 pound of pasta)

*Here's a way to take something simple and make it
look and taste fancy. Imagine . . . no fuss at all!!*

½ cup mayonnaise

1 cup (½ pint) half-and-half

¼ cup chopped fresh dill

2 medium-sized tomatoes,
finely chopped

1 scallion, finely chopped

1 teaspoon salt

¼ teaspoon pepper

In a saucepan, mix together the mayonnaise, half-and-half, and chopped dill; cook over medium heat, stirring occasionally, until the mixture is heated through. Remove from the stove; stir in the tomatoes, scallion, salt, and pepper.

NOTE: Serve immediately over spaghetti or your favorite pasta and sprinkle with grated Parmesan cheese, if desired.

# creamy spaghetti sauce

about 2¾ cups
(enough for 1 pound of pasta)

*There's a really smooth sauce that's popular in
Italian restaurants now—some call it Cream Sauce,
or Vodka Sauce, or Ravioli Sauce.
It's light and mild, so whatever you call it, you'll
look like you're right "up to the minute."*

1 container (15 ounces) ricotta
cheese (about 2 cups)

1 cup prepared spaghetti sauce

About ¼ cup milk

Vodka to taste (optional)

In a medium-sized bowl, combine the cheese and spaghetti sauce. Beat with an electric mixer on medium speed until smooth. Add the milk slowly, a little at a time, until the sauce is thinned to desired consistency. Add the vodka with the milk, if desired. Warm the sauce on the stove or in the microwave and serve.

NOTE: Serve over pasta or ravioli, whatever's your favorite. For a little different taste, try adding oregano or basil (2 tablespoons chopped fresh or 1 tablespoon dried) or a touch of cayenne pepper to make it hotter.

# tomato cream sauce

2½ cups

*There's always another way to enjoy pasta. I'll bet you haven't tried this combination yet. It's so rich and smooth.*

1 cup heavy cream

2 ounces (½ stick) butter

3 ounces (3 wedges) soft processed Gruyère cheese, like Laughing Cow®, Bon Bel®, or Tiger Brand®

1 cup warmed prepared spaghetti sauce

In a medium-sized saucepan or double boiler, combine the heavy cream, butter, and cheese. Cook over a low heat until everything is melted and the sauce is velvety smooth, about 20 minutes. Add the warmed spaghetti sauce, mix together, and use immediately.

NOTE: Serve over fettuccine or your favorite pasta. For some added crunch, add a 16-ounce bag of frozen cauliflower, broccoli, and carrot combination that has been thawed and blanched.

# lower-fat alfredo sauce

about 1 cup
(enough for ½ pound of fettuccine)

*You won't believe this is a lighter variation
of the popular sauce.*

1 cup skim milk

1 tablespoon imitation butter
granules

6 wedges low-fat processed
cheese, like Laughing Cow®

1 tablespoon grated Parmesan
cheese

Pinch of garlic powder

In a medium-sized saucepan or double boiler, combine all the ingredients until everything is melted and the sauce is velvety smooth, about 20 minutes. Serve immediately.

NOTE: Serve over fettuccine and, if you like, add half of a 16-ounce package of frozen cauliflower, broccoli, and carrot combination that has been thawed and blanched.

# bean sauce italia

about 1¼ cups

(enough for 1 to 2 pounds of pasta)

*Think this sounds like a crazy combination?*
*Taste it and you'll*
*agree that it's an easy, old-time taste that fits today.*

| | |
|---|---|
| ½ cup olive oil | 1 tablespoon lemon juice |
| 1 can (15 to 16 ounces) chick peas, drained | 1 teaspoon salt |
| | 1 teaspoon pepper |
| 5 garlic cloves, coarsely chopped | ½ teaspoon chili powder |

**P**lace the olive oil, chick peas, garlic, lemon juice, salt, pepper, and chili powder in a blender, in that order. (It will blend better.) Purée, mixing frequently with a spoon, until it becomes a paste.

NOTE: Enjoy this tossed with hot cooked pasta. It's also wonderful as a bread spread: Slice Italian bread lengthwise, brush with olive oil on both sides, bake at 375°F. for about 20 minutes, or until golden brown, and spread it with this.

# pesto sauce

about 1½ cups
(enough for 1 pound of pasta)

*For true Italian taste excitement, this is a fresh basil sauce
that's like eating right in the garden—and it's so versatile . . .
Use as a salad dressing, over pasta, or even over boiled
potatoes. However you use it, it's bound to get raves.*

2 cups fresh basil, lightly
packed

1 cup olive oil

1 cup grated Parmesan cheese

2 garlic cloves, crushed

1 teaspoon salt

½ cup pine nuts, almonds, or
walnuts, finely chopped

Dash of ground nutmeg
(optional)

**P**lace all the ingredients in a blender or food processor; blend
until smooth. Store in the refrigerator, covered, until ready to use.
Mix well before serving; use hot or cold.

# Index

index

# Get All Five Books
# in the Mr. Food® Library!

WILLIAM MORROW

# Mr. Food®

## Can Help You Be A Kitchen Hero!

### Let **Mr. Food**® make your life easier with
### Quick, No-Fuss Recipes and Helpful Kitchen Tips for

**Family Dinners • Soups and Salads • Potluck Dishes
Barbecues • Special Brunches • Unbelievable Desserts**

### . . . and that's just the beginning!

Complete your **Mr. Food**® cookbook library today.
It's so simple to share in all the
**"OOH IT'S SO GOOD!!"™**

✂ - - - - - - - - - - - - - - - - - - - - - - - - - - - - - - - - - - - - - - - - - - - - - - - - - - - - - - - - - - - - -

| TITLE | PRICE | QUANTITY | |
|---|---|---|---|
| A. **Mr. Food**® Cooks Like Mama | @ $12.95 each | x _____ | = $_____ |
| B. The **Mr. Food**® Cookbook, *OOH IT'S SO GOOD!!*™ | @ $12.95 each | x _____ | = $_____ |
| C. **Mr. Food**® Cooks Chicken | @ $ 9.95 each | x _____ | = $_____ |
| D. **Mr. Food**® Cooks Pasta | @ $ 9.95 each | x _____ | = $_____ |
| E. **Mr. Food**® Makes Dessert | @ $ 9.95 each | x _____ | = $_____ |
| F. **Mr. Food**® Cooks Real American | @ $14.95 each | x _____ | = $_____ |
| G. **Mr. Food**®'s Favorite Cookies | @ $11.95 each | x _____ | = $_____ |
| H. **Mr. Food**®'s Quick and Easy Side Dishes | @ $11.95 each | x _____ | = $_____ |
| I. **Mr. Food**® Grills It All in a Snap | @ $11.95 each | x _____ | = $_____ |
| J. **Mr. Food**®'s Fun Kitchen Tips and Shortcuts (and Recipes, Too!) | @ $11.95 each | x _____ | = $_____ |
| K. **Mr. Food**®'s Old World Cooking Made Easy | @ $14.95 each | x _____ | = $_____ |
| L. "Help, **Mr. Food**®! Company's Coming!" | @ $14.95 each | x _____ | = $_____ |
| M. **Mr. Food**® Pizza 1-2-3 | @ $11.95 each | x _____ | = $_____ |
| N. **Mr. Food**® Meat Around the Table | @ $11.95 each | x _____ | = $_____ |
| O. **Mr. Food**® Simply Chocolate | @ $11.95 each | x _____ | = $_____ |

**Call 1-800-619-FOOD (3663) or send payment to:**
**Mr. Food**®
P.O. Box 696
Holmes, PA 19043

Name _____

Street _____ Apt._____

City _____ State_____ Zip_____

Method of Payment: ☐ Check or Money Order Enclosed

☐ Credit Card:  ☐ Visa ☐ MasterCard  Expiration Date _____

Signature _____

Account #: ☐☐☐☐☐☐☐☐☐☐☐☐☐☐☐☐☐☐

| | |
|---|---|
| **Book Total** | $_____ |
| +$2.95 Postage & Handling First Copy *AND* $1 Ea. Add'l. Copy (Canadian Orders Add Add'l. $2.00 *Per Copy*) | $_____ |
| **Subtotal** | $_____ |
| Less $1.00 per book if ordering 3 or more books with this order | $ –_____ |
| *Add Applicable Sales Tax (FL Residents Only)* | $_____ |
| **Total in U.S. Funds** | $_____ |

Please allow 4 to 6 weeks for delivery.

BKD1